D0570908

*FOLLIES*
*AND*
*FANTASIES*

*Germany*
*and*
*Austria*

*HARRY N. ABRAMS, INC.*
Publishers

# FOLLIES AND FANTASIES

*Germany*

*and*

*Austria*

*Photographs*

*by Nic Barlow*

*Introduction by*

*Dale Harris*

*Text by*

*Sally Sample Aall*

*TO CHRISTIAN HIORTH AALL*

*Editor: Adele Westbrook*
*Designer: Elissa Ichiyasu*
*Photo Research: Neil Ryder Hoos*

*Library of Congress*
*Cataloging-in-Pub*
*Barlow, Nic.*
*Follies and fantasies:*
*Germany and Austria /*
*photographs by Nic Barlow ;*
*introduction by Dale Harris ;*
*text by Sally Sample Aall.*
*   p.   cm.*
*ISBN 0–8109–3323–3*
*1. Architecture, Domestic—Germany—*
*Pictorial works.*
*2. Follies (Architecture)—*
*Germany—Pictorial works.*
*3. Pavilions—Germany—Pictorial works.*
*4. Architecture, Modern—Germany—*
*Pictorial works.*
*5. Architecture, Domestic—Austria—*
*Pictorial works.*
*6. Follies (Architecture)—Austria—*
*Pictorial works.*
*7. Pavilions—Austria—Pictorial works.*
*8. Architecture, Modern—Austria—*
*Pictorial works.*
*I. Aall, Sally Sample, 1926–*
*II. Title.*
*NA7349.B36   1994*
*728'.9—dc20     93–50773*

*Photographs copyright © 1994*
*Nic Barlow*

*Introduction copyright © 1994*
*Dale Harris*

*Text copyright © 1994 Harry N. Abrams,*
*Inc.*

*Published in 1994 by Harry N. Abrams,*
*Incorporated, New York*
*A Times Mirror Company*
*All rights reserved.*
*No part of the contents of this book*
*may be reproduced without the written per-*
*mission of the publisher*
*Printed and bound in Japan*

# CONTENTS

# INTRODUCTION

*The Star Hunting Lodge, Sans Souci.*
*Potsdam, Germany. Staatliche Schlösser*
*und Gärten, Potsdam-San Souci*

The architecture commissioned by the nobility of Germany and Austria during the Ancien Régime—an architecture encompassing both the flamboyance of Baroque and the grace of Rococo—is less internationally celebrated than its contemporary counterparts in France and Britain. All the same, it deserves to be ranked alongside these as one of the most distinguished achievements in European culture.

Not only is its quality extraordinary, but much of it survives, the greater part in excellent condition. Though Europe has long since seen the end of the autocratic social order that produced so many magnificent palaces during the eighteenth century—not to mention the often exquisite pavilions, belvederes, and hunting lodges built on their grounds—the Germans and Austrians of more democratic times have taken great pains to preserve this important part of their cultural heritage (see page 8).

They have even managed to make up for a great deal of the destruction that occurred in World War II. In Munich, for example, the court theater designed by François Cuvilliés and built between 1751–53, is back in operation at the former royal palace of the Wittelsbachs, the Residenz, albeit in a location slightly different from its original one.

In 1945, when news about what had been going on in Germany during the recently concluded war began to circulate in the world outside, it was widely reported that the theater—which had seen the first performance of Mozart's *Idomeneo* in 1781 and, some 150 years later, was still in working order—had been destroyed in one of the Allied bombing raids that severely damaged the Residenz.

The rumor, however, was untrue. What had happened is that in 1944, when Munich was hit by a series of heavy air attacks, the auditorium, one of the most ravishing examples of Rococo decorative architecture in existence, was dismantled, packed in crates, and sent to a safe place until the end of hostilities. With the return of peace, the crates, which luckily had remained unharmed, were shipped back to Munich.

Between 1956–58, the beautifully carved and painted putti, herms, caryatids, allegorical figures, masks, coats of arms, crowns, shells, palm leaves, and simulated silk draperies were reassembled according to the

*The Pheasantry (southern view), Schloss Moritzburg. Dresden, Germany. Constructed 1763–82. Photo: Sächsische Landesbibliothek, Dresden*

*Belvedere on the Klausburg (destroyed), Sans Souci. Potsdam, Germany. Etching by A.L. Druger, 1776 (after painting by F. Meyer). Staatliche Schlösser und Gärten, Potsdam-Sans Souci*

Vue du Belvedére situé vers le Septentrion du Nouveau Palais de Sans Souci.

original plans of Cuvilliés in a newly created space inside the restored Residenz. With the installation of up-to-date stage machinery behind the proscenium arch, the theater began life all over again. Renamed the Cuvilliés Theater, in honor of its Walloon architect, it is once again a fully functioning opera house, though now used only on special occasions.

The resuscitation of the Residenz Theater is but one of the many examples of architectural revivification in post-war Germany and Austria. In Potsdam, Frederick the Great's elegant Sans Souci Palace, badly damaged by bombs, has been meticulously restored to its original condition. So has the major part of Berlin's Charlottenburg Palace, virtually the whole of which was gutted by fire in an air raid in 1943.

In Dresden, work has been completed on the rebuilding of the Zwinger, the ensemble of Baroque pavilions and arcades built for Elector Augustus the Strong of Saxony, and to all intents and purposes destroyed in the Allied air attacks of 1945. There is even talk that the Berlin Stadtschloss, the eclectic but largely Baroque Hohenzollern palace damaged during the war and then wantonly demolished in 1950 by the Communist government of East Germany, will eventually be reconstructed.

From Bremen in the north to Munich in the south, from Vienna in the east to Trier in the west, the German-speaking lands of Central Europe are filled with architectural marvels dating from the century immediately preceding the outbreak of the French Revolution in 1789: palaces, like Würzburg, with its cloud-capped

frescoes by Gian Battista Tiepolo; libraries, like Vienna's Hofbibliothek, over whose central hall floats a superbly proportioned dome, steeped in light and color; resplendent abbeys that dominate the surrounding countryside, like Melk on the Danube; tiny country churches, like Wies, in Bavaria, its exterior plain to a point of austerity, its interior luxuriant with ornamentation in a characteristic range of Rococo colors: pink, lime green, daffodil, azure, teal, blood red—the whole touched at salient points with gold.

As such buildings demonstrate, German and Austrian architecture of the Ancien Régime is marked by both elegance and profusion. The elegance derives quite naturally from the high level of aesthetic taste cultivated in the courts of Central Europe during this period, the profusion from the mania for building that took possession of the nobility during the latter portion of the seventeenth century and raged unchecked for the better part of a hundred years (see page 9). Only when the old social order was threatened by the French Revolution, in fact, did the aristocratic passion for building somewhat abate, although, even then, artistic standards remained as notable as ever (see page 10).

Until the effects of the Revolution were fully felt, an obsession with architecture remained a defining feature of the Ancien Régime in Central Europe. Obsession, though, is probably the wrong word for this phenomenon, since it implies unthinking fervor, and most of the princes who succumbed to the craze for building were anything but mindless in the pursuit of their aims.

One of the most interesting and knowledgeable of those in thrall to bricks and mortar was Lothar Franz von Schönborn, Arch-Chancellor of the Holy Roman Empire, Elector-Archbishop of Mainz, Prince-Bishop of Bamberg, and Canon of Würzburg, a man who declared himself to be at

the mercy of a *bauwurm*—a yearning to build so compulsive that it gnawed at him from within.

This compulsion he succumbed to by commissioning two vast and splendid palaces: one in Bamberg, the New Residence, where a stiffly impressive portrait of him in ecclesiastical robes topped by an ermine cape hangs today in the billiard room; and the other in Pommersfelden, near Bamberg, called Schloss Weissenstein, a building distinguished by its soaring marble salon and, above all, its light-filled, arcaded staircase-hall, one of the high points of Central European Baroque.

*The Dianaburg, Schloss Kranichstein. Darmstadt, Germany. Painting by Georg Adam Eger (1727–1808). Private collection. Jagdmuseum Schloss Kranichstein*

Grande Chasse donnée au Baerrensee près de Stuttgart, *Schloss Solitude. Stuttgart, Germany. Etching by Viktor Heideloff, 1782. Württembergische Landesbibliothek, Stuttgart*

When Lothar Franz's nephew and heir, Prince-Bishop Friedrich Karl von Schönborn, told his uncle about his plans for a summer palace in Lower Austria, the Arch-Chancellor wrote back to say that the news made his mouth water. Nevertheless, he was wise enough not to ruin himself by embarking on too many grand building schemes. As he once confessed, somewhat ruefully: "Building is a craze which costs much," adding, disarmingly, "but every fool likes his own hat."

The individuality of taste to which Lothar Franz here refers was not simply psychological in origin. In large measure, it stemmed from the rivalry of proudly independent rulers. While Austria had been a sovereign state since the thirteenth century, with the

advent of its first Habsburg potentate Rudolf I, Germany had never at any time achieved national unity. Indeed, during the Ancien Régime, it consisted of no fewer than 396 distinct and independent territories, each with its own ruler, and, as a matter of course, its own army, customs, laws, currency, taxes, and tariffs.

Although the world might refer to these territories collectively as Germany, the designation was, at best, a trope, even if a convenient one. Germany was not merely atomized, it was also highly diverse, consisting of powerful states such as Saxony (a kingdom since 1697) and Prussia (a kingdom since 1701), as well as a host of smaller, less assertive regions of many kinds. These included dukedoms, earldoms, counties, marquisates, principalities, bishoprics, electorates, and a group of so-called free Imperial cities, like Bremen,

Hamburg, and Lübeck, all of the latter being rich, proud, and resolutely independent.

"Imperial" here refers to the Holy Roman Empire, of which these territories, along with Austria, formed part. Despite the resplendent sound of its name, however, this institution, though ancient, was not an Empire in any practical sense. Indeed, it had no real political identity. Member states made alliances independently, and went to war without consulting one another, often ending up on opposing sides.

The only unifying influence was cultural and atavistic, consisting, above all, of a widespread belief in a shared distant past, a belief reinforced by the use throughout most of the territories of a common tongue. Even so, in Prussia, which by the end of the Ancien Régime had become the mightiest of the German-speaking states after Austria, the language of the court, and thus of the aristocracy as a whole, was French.

In any case, the forces ranged against the effective unification of the German lands were powerful. They included not merely secular rivalry but religious dissension, the latter of a violent kind. Just over a century after Martin Luther nailed his ninety-five theses to the door of the court church at Wittenberg in 1517, a savage war broke out between Catholics and Protestants.

As the conflict widened, the nature of the struggle changed: within a few years, co-religionists found themselves ranged against one another in a struggle that ultimately had more to do with secular ambition than with spiritual conviction. The fighting, which lasted from 1618–48, was unusually bloody, even for those sanguinary times, its destructive effects being felt for generations after the advent of peace.

Indeed, the Thirty Years' War, as it has come to be called, survives in collective memory as one of the most disastrous eras in the history of Central Europe—until World War II, in fact, the most disastrous of all. It is significant that Bertolt Brecht's uncompromisingly pacifistic play *Mother Courage*, written in 1939, should be set during that period of unchecked destructiveness.

While it raged, Germany became a virtual desert: flourishing cities were transformed into rubble, in which wolves foraged at will; productive arable and grazing lands reverted to wilderness; peasants and townsfolk alike were reduced to penury by the rapine of marauding troops; large numbers of people were annihilated through famine, and the plague that followed upon the latter as a matter of course. By the time the contenders signed the Peace of Westphalia in 1648, the population of Germany had fallen from sixteen to six million.

Recovery was slow. Incursions by Ottoman armies into Western Europe delayed the return of prosperity. The arts, uncultivated for decades by an aristocracy whose energies and resources had been devoted primarily

*The Pagodenburg, Schloss Rastatt. Rastatt, Germany. Photo: Foto Marburg/Art Resource, New York*

*The Belvedere for the Prince of Liechten-
stein, Palais Liechtenstein. Vienna, Austria.
Engraving.*

to aggression, defense, and the art of
survival, did not begin to show signs
of life again until after 1683, when the
Turks, having laid siege to Vienna,
were defeated by an army under the
command of John Sobieski, King of
Poland. Sixteen years later, the treaty
of Karlowitz signified an even more
decisive end to the Turkish threat.

In 1702, however, the return to full-
scale prosperity was again delayed by
the outbreak of hostilities, the War of
the Spanish Succession, which
arrayed the might of France under
Louis XIV against the greater part of
Europe, including Britain. Only with
the signing in 1714 of the Treaty of
Rastatt between the principal adver-
saries, France and Austria, would the
wholesale recovery of the German
states begin (see page 11).

During its long years of strife, Germany had seen very little building
activity of any consequence. Now,
with the renewal of confidence that
followed upon the return of peace,
came a yearning for expansiveness, for
tokens of stability and the trappings of
autocracy. At long last, the rulers of
Central Europe could raise monuments to their own magnificence.

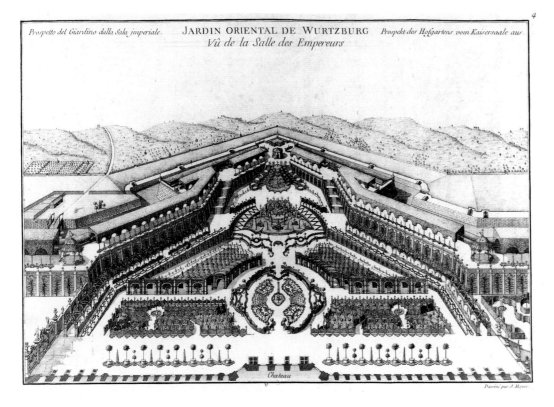

Prospetto del Giardino dalla Sala imperiale. JARDIN ORIENTAL DE WURTZBURG Prospekt des Hofgartens vom Kaisersaale aus. Vù de la Salle des Empereurs

Chateau

Dessiné par J. Mayer.

*Plan of the Oriental Garden (east garden), Würzburg. Würzburg, Germany. Engraving after Johann Prokop Mayer, 1773. Bayerische Verwaltung der Staatlichen Schlösser, Gärten und Seen, Schloss Nymphenburg, Munich*

What followed was an explosion of palace building without precedent in these lands. Some major projects had been initiated before the Treaty of Rastatt; their number increased prodigiously after the latter was signed.

Among the many splendid buildings that rose in the years before 1789 are Schönbrunn, the summer home of the Austrian Emperor, then outside the walls of Vienna; Solitude, near Stuttgart, built for Duke Karl Eugen of Württemberg (see page 12); Würzburg, built for Prince-Bishop Johann Philippe Franz von Schönborn; the red limestone castle of Rastatt, built for Margrave Ludwig Wilhelm of Baden, known to the world as Turkish Ludwig for his victories over the Ottoman armies; and the smaller, more lavishly decorated Favorite, begun by Turkish Ludwig's widow in 1710, three years after her husband's death.

Although each of these reveals a distinctive style of its own, all inevitably have in common the inspiration of Louis XIV's Versailles, the most celebrated, and emulated, royal residence in the world. Every aristocrat who could visit Versailles did so. Those who could not were nevertheless likely to be familiar with its architecture, its sumptuous decorations and its extensive, unprecedentedly grand gardens, through the reports of innumerable awestruck visitors. Thousands more scrutinized the many engravings that offered a dazzling impression of the château's manifold splendors.

Louis, at seventy-six (an unusually advanced age for the time) and with only a year to live after peace was signed in 1714 at Turkish Ludwig's recently completed castle of Rastatt (see page 13), did not emerge from the war with the victory he had sought. Though France ostensibly remained the greatest power in Europe, the country was, in actuality, financially ruined. Even so, its cultural and artistic influence continued to be immense. Versailles, in which the king sequestered himself after 1693, was not merely the most admired contemporary palace in the world, it was an awe-inspiring emblem of majesty, a manifestation in architectural terms of the triumph of absolutist principles.

*Ruin on right side of garden entrance,*
*Schloss Ludwigsburg. Ludwigsburg,*
*Germany. Plan by Nette, c. 1709.*
*Schlossverwaltung Ludwigsburg, Staatliche*
*Schlösser und Gärten, Heimatmuseum,*
*Ludwigsburg*

As such, it could have no rivals in France, unless, that is, the King should suddenly have taken it into his head to surpass himself. Certainly, none of the aristocracy, however rich, built anything of real substance in Louis's later years. Long before Versailles took on its definitive form during the 1680s, after many years of construction, palace building elsewhere in the country had virtually come to an end.

The reason is quite obvious: During the early years of his reign, Louis had decisively crushed the power of the French aristocracy, which had attempted to assert its ancient privileges in the face of the monarchy's determination to affirm its own supremacy. The nobles, decisively defeated in battle, finally came to terms with their subjugation to the throne. As a result, they had no need to build, or rebuild, palaces in order to affirm their status, this being now defined largely in terms of their subservient relationship to the all-powerful monarch, upon whom they danced attendance as courtiers at Versailles.

Matters were very different in Germany, where the nominal head of the Empire, almost invariably the ruler of Austria, exercised no such sway over its constituent members. These, in any case, were sovereign rulers, unbeholden to anyone, for which reason they were subject to none of the constraints that kept the French from palace building.

After enduring thirty years of barbaric warfare and its sometimes even more appalling consequences, they were ready to reassert the principles of civilized behavior, long held in abeyance, and to show themselves to the world as exemplars of enlightenment. The ideal medium for their ambitions was architecture, at once an exemplification of their social position, their effective power, and their regard for the arts. A handsome new palace, moreover, was an opportunity literally to remake one's world, to start, as it were, afresh.

Though these rulers took Versailles as the starting point for their new palaces, they did not necessarily want a slavish copy of it. For one thing, its scale and opulence were beyond the means of most German princelings. (Even Louis had to sacrifice the silver furniture of Versailles in order to pay for his increasingly ruinous wars.) For another, both the architecture and decorations of Versailles were couched in a stylistic idiom that by the beginning of the eighteenth century had begun to seem too heavy-handed, ceremonial, and overbearing.

Nevertheless, it was to France that Central Europeans looked for guidance in most cultural matters. Long after the death of *le grand monarque*, in fact, France continued to dominate the imagination of Europe. Not only was the language of Frederick the

*The Rock Garden and Oriental Pavilion, Sanspareil. Bayreuth, Germany. Engraving, 1746–47. Bayerische Verwaltung der Staatlichen Schlösser, Gärten und Seen, Schloss Nymphenburg, Munich*

Vue du Batiment Principal : Eremite a Sanspareil. | Prospect von dem haupt Eremite Gebaude zu Sanspareil.
avec Privilege de Son Altesse Serene Margrave de Brandenbg Bayreuth.

Great's court French, so was its cultural bent. Although he eventually quarrelled irrevocably with Voltaire, Frederick did not rest until he had persuaded the French philosopher to visit him in Prussia, where Voltaire remained the monarch's guest from 1750-53. (The French, incidentally, reciprocated the King's admiration, being the first to dub Frederick "the Great.") Diderot exercised a similar fascination on Catherine the Great of Russia, with whom he corresponded and whose capital he visited, and on Joseph II, the Austrian and Holy Roman Emperor (with whom he also corresponded).

Not surprisingly, a large number of the distinguished architects who worked in Germany and Austria during the Ancien Régime were French, among them: Charles Philippe Dieussart, Joseph St. Pierre, Pierre-Louis-Philippe de la Guêpière, Jean-Nicolas Jadot de Ville Issey, Nicolas de Pigage, and Jean-Laurent Legeay. They were joined by large numbers of their fellow-countrymen who worked as stuccoists, masons, engineers, gardeners and landscape architects, all drawn eastward by a demand for their services, which their financially ruined native land could no longer afford.

By the end of the seventeenth century, Versailles was an emblem both of absolute power and of the privileges that flowed from it. Increasingly oppressed by the rigorous formality of life at the great château, where the rituals of kingship and the maintenance of daily life required the services of some 25,000 people, and where even his morning awakening from sleep and his nightly retirement to bed were public ceremonies, Louis in 1670 commissioned the architect Louis Le Vau to design him a *maison de plaisance*, a pleasure pavilion, in the nearby village of Trianon.

What Louis wanted was a retreat, small and relatively simple, where he could conduct himself according to his personal inclinations rather than his public obligations. Here, released from the formal restrictions of an elaborate courtly existence, the monarch could entertain his intimates with almost as much freedom as though he were a private citizen.

*The Gardens at Steinfort (Westphalia). Steinfort, Germany. Engraving from G. Le Rouge,* Details des Nouveaux Jardins à La Monde, *1774–89. British Architectural Library, RIBA, London*

*Das Boudoir (destroyed), Schloss Hohenheim. Stuttgart, Germany. Print, 1796.*

Above all, he could dally without constraint with his mistress, Madame de Montespan.

Graced with a blue-and-white faience roof, apparently inspired by the porcelain pagoda at Nanking, the Trianon de Porcelaine, as Louis's rural sanctuary was named, anticipated by more than fifty years the vogue for Chinoiserie that swept over Europe during the eighteenth century. But the building enjoyed only a short life, being pulled down in 1687, five years after Louis replaced Madame de Montespan with Madame de Maintenon, the governess of his seven children by the former.

By then, *le grand monarque* wanted a refuge of a more capacious and splendid kind, although one still markedly simpler than Versailles itself. The result was the Trianon de Marbre, the Marble Trianon, known today as the Grand Trianon. This, like the pavilion it replaced, represented a conscious flight from ritual and pomp, but one that entailed no loss of elegance or of exquisite workmanship.

In 1679, work began on a further retreat, a complex of buildings at Marly, also in the vicinity of Versailles. Here Jules Hardouin-Mansart, the architect of the Grand Trianon, built the King a small, luxurious pavilion flanked by twelve smaller guest houses for his close friends, with whom, attended by a suitable number of servants, he could withdraw, usually on weekends, from the gaze of the world.

Despite what is bound to strike us today as their regal sumptuousness, the relative modesty and informality of Marly and the Grand Trianon signified an acknowledgment that, although the monarch might wield absolute power, he was susceptible to the same basic emotional needs as the humblest of his subjects. With the construction of Louis's retreats, absolutism bent the knee to human fallibility.

Today, the distinction between a palace designed as a theater in which the monarch enacts the ceremonies of rulership in full view of his court, and a pavilion designed for the satisfaction of his private inclinations, is not always immediately apparent. Marly is no longer extant, but both Versailles and the Grand Trianon are now museums (although the latter is also used on occasion to house important foreign dignitaries on official business in France). As a result, the original function of these buildings has been obscured by their status as historic monuments.

While Versailles is very much grander in scale—as well as more majestic in character—than the Grand Trianon, the latter, with its marble columns and elegant interiors (much changed from what they were in Louis's time, however), looks so splendid to present-day eyes that it is hard to realize how

*The Indian House and Gardens (destroyed in 1822), Augustusburg Park. Brühl, Germany. Painting by François Rousseau, c. 1760. Rheinisches Amt für Denkmalpflege, Bonn*

fundamentally dissimilar the spirit permeating the two buildings must have seemed to Louis's contemporaries.

That they were perfectly aware of the difference between the character of the palace and of the Grand Trianon is evident from the number of pleasure pavilions inspired by the latter all over Europe (see page 14). The Grand Trianon, along with its predecessor (known outside France through contemporary engravings), became the prototype of the intimate edifices that the majority of German rulers henceforth felt obliged to include in their building plans, whether they had mistresses to entertain in them or not.

As everyone recognized, implicit in the architecture of Versailles was not merely authority but responsibility—the obligation to rule as wisely as possible. Louis's bedroom was placed in the very center of the château, not merely to enable him to survey the entire estate from his windows, but also because the arrangement provided so telling a metaphor of the absolute power invested in his person.

The same metaphor guided the plans of Hardouin-Mansart at Marly, where the King's pavilion occupied the middle of the site, and the lodgings of his relatives and friends the periphery. This arrangement echoed the relationship of the planets to the sun, the very emblem of the King, who was known as the *Roi Soleil*, and never forgot his exalted status, even before his intimates.

The metaphorical force of Marly was not lost on the princes of Central Europe. At Clemenswerth, the hunting lodge built near Sögel between 1736–50 by Clemens August, the Elector-Archbishop of Cologne and Bishop of Münster and Paderborn, the Elector's two-story octagonal pavilion was surrounded by eight buildings, seven one-story pavilions for courtiers and servants, and a somewhat grander three-story pavilion that housed a chapel.

Despite the fact that it gave unmistakable architectural expression to the autocratic ideal, Marly, like the Grand Trianon, represented the conscious abdication of responsibility, albeit a momentary one. Both Marly and the Trianons were essentially acts of self-indulgence, of the assertion of private need over kingly duty. Significantly enough, none was ever meant to be seen by the world at large, merely by those closest to the monarch.

At least one Central European ruler who emulated Louis had first-hand knowledge of life at Versailles. The Elector Max Emanuel of Bavaria, having thrown in his lot with the French in the War of the Spanish Succession, went down to defeat with them in 1704 at the battle of Blenheim, and was forced by the victorious Austrians and British to abandon his throne. Settling first in Brussels, he eventually moved closer to Louis, living for some years thereafter in Saint-Cloud, outside Paris. In 1714, he was restored to his lands by the Treaty of Rastatt, a bounty the

*The Indian House, Augustusburg Park. Brühl, Germany. Engraving, c. 1755.*

French monarch won for his old ally during the peace negotiations.

Shortly before his setback at Blenheim forced him out of Bavaria, Max Emanuel had sent Josef Effner, the talented son of his chief gardener, to Paris in order to study with the architect Germain Boffrand, the greatest master of Rococo in France. When the Elector was restored to his throne, he appointed Effner court architect, putting him in charge of the refurbishment of Nymphenburg, his summer palace outside Munich. In carrying out this task, Effner clearly had the example of Versailles before his eyes.

Not only was Nymphenburg enlarged and decoratively enriched—with the result that it looked more clearly like the residence of a powerful autocrat—so were the grounds, all of the changes to the latter being effected in the style of Versailles. To take charge of these alterations, Max Emanuel appointed a Frenchman, Dominique Girard, who transformed what had been an elaborate Italian garden into a French ornamental park, no less formal but more rational and elegant. With its clipped trees, parterres, flower beds, canals, *allées,* and long vistas, it was an extension into the world of nature of the same principles expressed by the palace itself, an alfresco setting for the highly ritualized ceremonies of court life.

As Hippolyte Taine said of the eighteenth-century French garden: "The parterres and parks are in reality an

*Steam Engine House, Sans Souci. Potsdam, Germany. Staatliche Schlösser und Gärten, Potsdam-Sans Souci*

open-air salon: nothing there is natural; everything has been arranged and corrected with social discourse in mind; there is no spot in which one can be alone or relaxed; it is a place for strolling in the company of others and greeting one's friends. These clipped yews represent vases and lyres. These parterres are simply carpets with a leafy design. In these calm and rectilinear paths, the King, with a staff in his hand, gathers around him his entire retinue." (See page 15.)

But the park at Nymphenburg was also the setting for more personal pleasures. On either side of the long canal, which, as at Versailles, established the central axis of the garden, Effner built a *maison de plaisance.* First came the Pagodenburg (1716-19), a teahouse and refreshment pavilion containing a pair of charming rooms in the Chinese taste, in which Max Emanuel could relax with his companions after the exertions of the hunt. Across from this, he then built the Badenburg (1719-21), a bathing pavilion, containing a heated swimming pool and a gallery for spectators, a building that, by its very nature, was open only to those intimate with the Elector.

A third pavilion, a hermitage known as the Magdalenenklause, which Effner started on in 1725, was conceived with more solitary pleasures in mind. Dedicated to the penitential Mary Magdalene, and designed to inculcate a spirit of otherworldliness, the Magdalenenklause was built to look like a ruin, a deliberate reminder of mortality and mutability.

Inside the building, Effner created four austerely furnished rooms, all

*The Mirror Room in the Schloss Favorite. Rastatt, Germany. Photo: Landesbildstelle Baden, Karlsruhe*

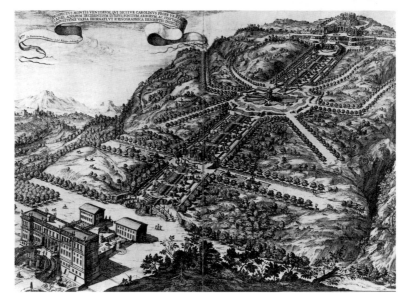

*Plan for the Karlsburg project. Kassel, Germany. Print by G. F. Guerniero, 1706. Staatliche Museen zu Berlin–Preussischer Kulturbesitz: Kunstbibliothek*

*The Palm House (interior), Peacock Island. Berlin, Germany. Painting by Carl Blechen. Staatliche Schlösser und Gärten, Potsdam-Sans Souci*

*The Tahitian Room in the Ruined Palace, Peacock Island. Berlin, Germany. Staatliche Schlösser und Gärten, Berlin. Photo: Jorg P. Anders.*

lined with stained oak, and a grotto-like chapel and anteroom, the walls and ceilings of these being covered with sea shells, pebbles, and tufa. The decorations of the Magdalenenklause, graceful exercises in mock-primitivism, were intended to summon up thoughts of the caves in which the religious hermits of old, like the Desert Fathers, passed their days in prayer and the mortification of the flesh.

Whether Max Emanuel ever intended to use the Magdalenenklause as an incentive to spiritual advancement is hard to determine. What is clear is that the Elector, one of the most notorious libertines of his time, showed

little inclination toward the self-abnegation that characterized the lives of the Desert Fathers. In any case, he died in 1726, two years before the building was finally completed. More certain than his religious sincerity is the likelihood that he commissioned a hermitage for the park at Nymphenburg, despite the fact that there was nothing comparable at Versailles, simply to keep up with the latest fashions in court architecture.

For, although Louis XIV himself was largely impervious to them, new concepts had begun to dominate the outlook of Europe by the time of the monarch's death in 1715. The fact that Enlightenment ideas became so universally accepted during the course of the eighteenth century no doubt led to a complementary interest

in areas of thought and feeling that lay beyond the domain of reason: irrationality, the occult, the more shadowy regions of the human psyche. At the very time when the Baroque, with its emphasis on delight, opulence, and energy, was at its zenith in Central Europe, there developed a vogue for building styles that expressed mystery, austerity, and introspection, especially of a melancholy kind.

Not that anyone ever thought that sham ruins or sham Gothic, the two most popular styles for such buildings, should displace the Baroque, merely that they could add spice to it. While it seems unlikely that any eighteenth-century ruler but Catherine the Great of Russia would have resolved to commission an entire residential complex in sham Gothic—as she did at Tsaritsyno, on the outskirts of Moscow—many other autocrats were susceptible enough to contemporary ideas to adopt an anti-Baroque mode for at least one of the pavilions in their palace grounds (see page 16).

Essentially, such structures were *jeux d'esprit*, social theaters in which their owners could assume roles incompatible with the formal demands of courtly life. Despite their connotations of transitoriness, the "ruins" were, for the most part, built to last. The Medievalism, too, was less tectonic than scenic, a species of decor that hardly ventured beyond battlements and the pointed arch, all of it in the "Gothick" style eventually to be brought to a climax in England by Horace Walpole. Even Catherine abandoned Tsaritsyno before it was anywhere near complete.

Nevertheless, the thoughts inspired by such adventures in mood-setting were clearly congenial to those who lived during the period immediately before the French Revolution, when the aristocracy, not yet called to account, felt free to indulge in costly games of make-believe. The sham dairy built for Marie Antoinette at the Hameau in Versailles, where, dressed in silk, she could pretend to be a milkmaid, is only the most famous of these ventures into social fantasy, which enabled the high-born to reach beyond their milieu without actually leaving it.

At parties given by Prince Georg Wilhelm, Margrave of Bayreuth, and his wife Sophia, for example, the guests would often divert themselves by dressing up as hermits. In 1715, the Prince went so far as to commission the architect Johann David Ränz to build him a hermitage, a group of buildings consisting of a cloister surrounded by a refectory, a grotto, and cells—the last clearly intended for party games and role-playing rather than for religious meditation.

Thirty years later, such buildings were still in fashion. In 1746, Frederick the

*The Schinkel Pavilion, Charlottenburg Park. Berlin, Germany. Staatliche Schlösser und Gärten, Berlin. Photo: Jorg P. Anders.*

*The Tent Room in the Schloss Charlottenhof,
Sans Souci. Potsdam, Germany. Staatliche
Schlösser und Gärten, Potsdam-Sans Souci*

Great's sister, Margravine Wilhelmine
of Bayreuth, commissioned a garden
for her palace of Sanspareil that fea-
tured an elaborate hermitage, as well
as dark caverns and lowering cliffs.
Despite such sober elements, it is
apparent that the garden was meant
to be more titillating than awe-
inspiring, since the principal feature of the hermitage consisted of a
"Hall of Coolness," a grotto-like
room containing trick fountains
designed to surprise the visitor with
sudden jets of water. While it is, of
course, possible these were intended
to impress Wilhelmine's guests with
the conviction that life is at best
uncertain, the more likely explanation
for them is that the Margravine was
simply trying to amuse her guests.

All projects of this kind, in fact, seem
to have been undertaken with no
loftier aim than to impart pleasure
through the creation of fantasy. The
same intention lies behind the pavilions in the Chinese taste that began to
proliferate in Central Europe during
the eighteenth century (see page 17).
Like mock ruins and the "Gothick,"
chinoiserie gave harmless expression
to a widespread wish to transcend the
limits of Enlightenment certainty. In
paying homage to the exotic, however,
the age succeeded in reaffirming its
sense of self-sufficiency.

Like the hermitages of the time, those
buildings that made reference to
Asian architecture and decorative
styles never went beyond the scenic
and the picturesque (see page 19).
Moreover, even at the height of a
vogue that embraced the Japanese

and the Indian as well as the Chinese—all equally inauthentic, but
charming, nonetheless—recourse to
the exotic was largely incidental (see
page 18). It was only, after all, in one
of the 452 rooms of Schloss Ludwigsburg, near Stuttgart, that Duke Eberhard of Württemberg installed a
series of Chinese-style lacquer panels,
and even here the framing of the panels is unambiguously Baroque in
character.

One of the few exceptions to the ten-
dency to relegate chinoiserie to a sub-
ordinate position in a larger
decorative scheme occurred at Wilhelmshöhe, near Kassel, where in
1781 Frederick II, Landgrave of Kassel built an entire village in the Chinese style, consisting of a farmhouse,
bungalows, a barn, stables, cowsheds,
and a ballroom-cum-dining room.
Although Moulang, as the Landgrave
called the village, had all the ear-
marks of a folly, Frederick's intention
was actually to create a functioning
dairy farm. As might have been pre-
dicted, the discrepancy between decorative fantasy and workaday
practicality ensured the speedy failure
of his scheme and the subsequent disappearance of all traces of the village.

Most evocations of Asia, however,
were both more modest in scale and
less practical in intention, such as the
Snail Shell and Indian House, set in
the park of Schloss Augustusburg in
Brühl, near Cologne. Both, like

*The Winter Garden (destroyed) at the Hofgarten side of the Residenz. Munich, Germany. Nineteenth-century photograph. Photo: Bayerische Verwaltung der Staatlichen Schlösser, Gärten und Seen, Schloss Nymphenburg, Munich*

Moulang, disappeared a long time ago, the former around 1776, the latter in 1822 (see page 20). Contemporary prints and paintings suggest that they must have given their builder, the Elector Clemens August of Cologne, son of Max Emanuel of Bavaria, much harmless pleasure.

The Snail Shell, a tiny four-story belvedere set in the middle of an ornamental pond, was girdled by a pair of curving outside staircases, and surmounted by a cupola in the form of a whorl. The Indian House, to which the Snail Shell was connected by a canal, was larger and more elaborate, a fanciful evocation, despite its name, of the Imperial Palace in Peking, consisting of three pavilions linked by galleries. Set in the midst of a formal garden that contained a pheasantry, it was clearly a colorful and joyous sight, the middle pavilion being red and pink, the side pavilions yellow and blue, and the roof green, with gold decorations (see page 21).

More modest yet is the still-extant Pagodenburg, the exotic pavilion built by Clemens August's father, Max Emanuel, at Nymphenburg. Although its name suggests an attempt to emulate the architecture of China, the building, well preserved today, is a determinedly Baroque building that simply happens to contain two rooms on the second floor decorated in the exotic style, one lined with gold-toned Chinese wallpaper, the other with red japanned panels. The ceilings of both are painted with oriental motifs. So are the outsides of the doors, although, unlike the diversely colored ceilings, these are in blue and white, obviously in order to match the unexotic Delft tiles that line the upper hall.

A similar conjunction of elements can be found at Falkenlust, the hunting pavilion in the grounds of Schloss Augustusburg, where a room exquisitely decorated with lacquer panels in black and gold, leads to a hallway lined with blue-and-white tiles bearing the device of the Wittelsbachs, the family that produced the builder of the pavilion, Clemens August. The

*The Royal Hunting Lodge, Jagdschloss Schachen. Schachen-Partenkirchen, Germany. Bayerische Verwaltung der Staatlichen Schlösser, Gärten und Seen, Schloss Nymphenburg, Munich*

latter, whose presence is felt throughout Schloss Augustusburg, is to be seen above the fireplace of Falkenlust's Lack Kabinett in a portrait of 1725. Clad in a turban and magnificent silk dressing gown, he holds a porcelain cup and saucer, just as he must have done when taking tea within these very walls.

Part of the charm of Central European Baroque and Rococo architecture is that none of such excursions into the exotic reveals the slightest self-consciousness about incongruity, just as none reveals the slightest concern for stylistic accuracy (see page 22). In the Badenburg at Nymphenburg, the bedroom mixes Chinese panoramic wallpaper with crystal chandeliers, Rococo stucco coving,

and occidental furniture, albeit furniture upholstered with oriental designs.

In the so-called Old Castle, outside Bayreuth, Margravine Wilhelmine installed a Japanese Room, most of whose decorative motifs are actually

*The Moorish Pavilion, Schloss Linderhof. Linderhof, Germany. Photo taken in 1934. Bayerische Verwaltung der Staatlichen Schlösser, Gärten und Seen, Schloss Nymphenburg, Munich*

Chinese. In the castle's Chinese Room, the main decorative feature consists of framed fragments of mirror placed in deliberately helter-skelter fashion all over the walls, possibly in order to evoke an exotic atmosphere through the disorientation of the viewer, whose sense of space the multiple reflections thus confound.

A similar decorative scheme can be found in the Spiegel Kabinett, the Mirror Room, of Schloss Favorite, though here the mirrors, while numerous as well as diverse in size and shape, are ranged around the room in a more comprehensible manner (see page 23). That the Spiegel Kabinett might always have been considered exotic as well as fantastic, however, is suggested by the presence of several blue-and-white Chinese pots on gilt brackets, though these form only a small part of the overall decorative scheme.

Mirrors play a no less disorienting role in the central salon of the Amalienburg, a small hunting pavilion in the grounds of Nymphenburg built by Cuvilliés for Amalia, the wife of Max Emanuel's son, Karl Albrecht. While the exterior of the pavilion is chastely Neo-Classical, the interiors, in the Rococo style, are as dazzling as the same architect's theater in the Munich Residenz, though lighter and more joyous in spirit. In the centrally placed blue-and-silver Spiegel Saal, one is plunged into an almost aquatic world of shifting light and ever-changing reflections, a dream-like, poetical atmosphere, in the midst of which the formal obligations of court life must have seemed blessedly remote.

That such a pavilion was meant to be understood as an accessory of the main building, the clear center of autocratic power, was more evident before the grounds of Nymphenburg were redesigned in the mid-eighteenth century and the French ornamental park replaced by a more naturalistic English garden. Originally, Amalienburg, Pagodenburg, and Badenburg, surrounded by their own geometrical gardens, stood at the focal point of the *allées* that cut across the park, and were visible from the parterre of the palace. Only the Magdalenenklause, designed to look lonely and even secret, was hidden from sight. So, today, are the other pavilions.

The rage for the English garden, which had conquered all of northern

*The Moorish Room in the Schloss Schachen-Partenkirchen. Schachen-Partenkirchen, Germany. 1871. Photo: Bayerische Verwaltung der Staatlichen Schlösser, Gärten und Seen, Schloss Nymphenburg, Munich*

Europe, including Russia, by the last decade of the eighteenth century, brought an end to such comprehensive formal landscaping schemes as the one created at the beginning of that century by Giovanni Francesco Guerniero for Landgrave Karl of Hesse, which utilized the entire hillside facing the latter's new palace at Wilhelmshöhe, eight miles from Kassel (see page 23).

Even with the vast changes made to the grounds in the mid-eighteenth century, these remain among the obligatory sights of Europe, animated as they are by a prodigious array of fountains, pools, grottoes, caves, bridges, temples, and artificial ruins. At the summit of the cascade sits an octagonal pavilion surmounted by a

pyramid, on the top of which towers a giant copper statue of Hercules. This, taken from the marble once owned by the Farnese family and now in the museum at Naples, is over thirty feet high. Hercules's club can hold eight people.

Impressive as the gardens of Schloss Wilhelmshöhe are today, they were once even grander. In the original plans of Guerniero, the hillside was sweepingly organized by a series of ascending terraces, each of which had its distinctive architectural feature: a belvedere, a temple, a pavilion, a fountain, and a basin. From the top of the hill, crowned by a magnificent octagonal pavilion set upon a grotto base, a vast water staircase led down to the garden behind the palace.

No one seeing all this—and it would have been possible to take in the whole panorama at a single glance—could have doubted the political authority of Landgrave Karl or his immediate successors. After the garden's transformation, the authority of the Landgraves of Hesse was harder to apprehend from their milieu, since the English approach produces gardens dominated not by comprehensiveness but by an almost anecdotal picturesqueness, in which the details are of far greater importance than the ensemble.

The autocratic world of the Ancien Régime came to an end, in effect, with the storming of the Bastille. The social and political changes that followed in the wake of the latter affected the extent of patronage available henceforth to architects, gardeners, and artists. It also affected taste, although Central Europe continued to prove susceptible to French aesthetic influence even after the invasion of German territories by the troops of, first, the new republic and then, in 1806, of Napoleon's Empire.

Long before the decisive defeat of the Emperor of the French at the Battle of Leipzig in 1813, a new nationalist sentiment had begun to stir among the German territories, and with it a new sobriety. Baroque and Rococo gave way to the sterner mode of Neo-Classicism. Fantasy and the pursuit of pleasure did not disappear from the courts of Central Europe, but it was expressed with less confidence, a growing awareness that aristocratic extravagance was likely to be met by criticism rather than by admiration. Among the rulers of Germany, the number of whom remained high, none—at least, until the middle of the nineteenth century—seems to have felt the gnawing of Lothar Franz's *bauwurm*.

They could not, in any case, afford to acknowledge such urges. In an age that saw the gradual replacement of autocracy by constitutional forms of government, the ruler now needed to solicit funds from his ministers before embarking on any costly project. As a result, he found he could indulge himself only on a comparatively modest scale.

Thus, pleasure pavilions, more affordable than palaces, continued to be built, even frivolous-looking ones. In 1797, the royal carpenter designed a mock ruin on Peacock Island in the Havel River for the King of Prussia, Karl Friedrich Wilhelm II. This small palace, still one of the sights of Greater Berlin, consists of a pair of towers (one of them lacking a crown) linked by a cast-iron bridge, below which stands a seemingly tumble-down wall. Despite the Romantic appearance of the exterior, the rooms inside are among the most fastidious examples of Neo-Classical design and workmanship in Europe. Even so, Romanticism found its way inside the castle too: one of the rooms is decorated in "Tahitian" style (see page 24). Alas, the Palm House, with its charming evocation of the Middle East, was burned down in 1880 (see page 24).

The same fastidiousness one finds in the interiors of the Peacock Island palace is visible in both the exterior and interior of the Neo-Classical pavilion erected in 1825 on the grounds of Charlottenburg Castle by Karl Friedrich Schinkel. By comparison with the pleasure pavilions of the former century, Schinkel's building represents no loss of elegance, only of decorative ostentation (see page 25).

Schinkel, whose versatility, stylistic range and technical skills place him in the forefront of German architects, was a master decorator as well as builder. Although his blue-and-white striped Tent Room in Schloss Charlottenhof (a small villa on the grounds of Frederick the Great's palace of Sans Souci) is marked by a sobriety characteristic of both the age and the designer's temperament, it displays an imaginative reach no less daring than that possessed by the great Baroque designers of the eighteenth century (see page 26). Deliberately confounding the ideas of stability and impermanence, Schinkel created a fantasy that any child who ever tried to create a hiding place inside his room would recognize as brilliant.

Neo-Classical restraint represented a swing of the pendulum that was bound in due course to reverse its direction. In both scale and manner, the greatest follies of the nineteenth century revert to the ebullience of the

*Hunding's Hut and Royal Sled (constructed in 1876, destroyed in 1884), Schloss Linderhof. Linderhof, Germany. Watercolor by H. Breling, 1882. Bayerische Verwaltung der Staatlichen Schlösser, Gärten und Seen, Schloss Nymphenburg, Munich*

Baroque (see page 27). These are the castles, pavilions, kiosks, grottoes, and indoor gardens created by Ludwig II of Bavaria during the final two decades of his life, which ended in 1886, when the king was found drowned in the Lake of Starnberg under circumstances no one has ever been able to explain satisfactorily.

In Ludwig, Lothar Franz's *bauwurm* reappears, more insatiable than ever (see page 28). The King, whose need for architectural and decorative settings in which he could escape from mundane reality and immerse himself in the life of the imagination, managed to keep his censorious, frugal-minded government at bay until almost the end. Millions of Bavarian marks went into the actualization of his fantasies (see pages 29, 30, and 31), which ranged from the Medieval (Neuschwanstein Castle) to the Baroque (the palaces of Linderhof and Herrenchiemsee), the Oriental (the Moorish kiosk in the park at Linderhof), and the Wagnerian (Hunding's Hut and Tannhäuser's Grotto, both at Linderhof).

Today, Bavaria reaps immense rewards from Ludwig's architectural follies, which attract thousands of paying visitors each year. Ludwig, of course, has had the last laugh, although only an unbalanced man would have attempted what he did under the increasingly egalitarian conditions of the time. When in 1906 the art-loving Grand Duke Ernst Ludwig of Hesse (brother of Alexandra, Empress of Russia) decided to commemorate his second marriage by raising a tower in his capital city of Darmstadt, he proceeded with the financial caution of a ruler who understood the democratic spirit of

the age. At once a prudent ruler and an architectural connoisseur, he gave the commission to Josef Maria Olbrich, thus ensuring his own lasting renown.

Twelve years later, in the wake of World War I, the rulers of Germany were swept away, seemingly forever, by a republican tide. Follies and architectural fantasies are an unlikely indulgence nowadays. Governments set their sights, not always successfully, on thrift and utility. Millionaires, who have filled some of the gaps left by the disappearance of Europe's rulers and nobles, prefer to spend their excess funds on paintings rather than on architecture. If they want to live in palaces, they no longer build them, they buy them ready-made.

*The Venus Grotto (interior) and King Ludwig's Shell-boat, Schloss Linderhof. Linderhof, Germany. Bayerisch Verwaltung der Staatlichen Schlösser, Gärten und Seen, Schloss Nymphenburg, Munich*

The Wedding Tower. Darmstadt, Germany.
Photo: Foto Marburg/Art Resource, New
York

*Admont, Austria*

## THE LUSTHAUS AT ADMONT ABBEY

*1*

The Benedictine Abbey of Admont in Styria was founded in 1074 by the Archbishop of Salzburg. It became a cultural center whose influence was felt far beyond its small market town surroundings in the Enns Valley. The Abbey is sited near the *Gesäuse* (the Roar), which takes its name from a wooded gorge ten miles long through which the river Enns plunges down some 500 feet between rugged escarpments.

The Abbey was badly damaged by fire in 1865, but fortunately the Baroque library survived with its valuable archives, consisting of 150,000 volumes, including 1,100 manuscripts and 900 early printed books. It has since been completely rebuilt. The library houses a State Room extending for seventy-five yards on either side of a central rotunda under a domed ceiling painted by Bartolommeo Altomonte. It is a fitting repository for this outstanding collection.

Shown here is the Abbey's *Lusthaus,* or folly.

*1*

## THE SWISS HOUSE
2

The Anholt Castle has had a turbulent history. Located in the lower Rhine valley, it is one of the many *Wasserburgen,* or water-surrounded fortresses, dotting this area, which trace their origins back to early Medieval strongholds. It was first documented in 1169 as a vassalage to the Utrecht Bishopric, but became independent and directly subordinated to the Emperor in the fourteenth century. During the following centuries, its masters became involved in a seemingly endless series of conflicts, from the Guelders feud to the Thirty Years' War, and the Castle was repeatedly invaded, looted, and occupied by enemy troops. Finally, in 1815, Anholt ceased to be an independent state and was incorporated into Prussia. Throughout those 700 years, the Castle remained in the hands of the same family, concluding with the Princes of Salm-Salm.

The Castle ensemble, reflecting all the architectural styles of its long life, is finished in red brick, forming a stunning contrast to the greenery and the blue water surrounding it. It sits in a large, rather informal garden containing a charming pavilion called the Swiss House, which is shown here.

2

## Schönbusch Park

*THE BANQUETING HALL AND THE LIGHTHOUSE*

3

*THE BANQUETING HALL*

4

3

4

Schönbusch, one of the earliest Classical gardens in Germany, was laid out for the Elector and Archbishop of Mainz to enhance the setting for a hunting lodge he built in 1778. An artificial lake with an island gave a clear view of the Renaissance Palace of Aschaffenburg across the Main river. Boats and gondolas plied the lake and a number of shepherds' huts with thatched roofs, as well as a miniature village of Dutch cottages, provided Romantic details that were added as a contrast to the more imposing Classical monuments. Several of these small buildings survive. The *Freundschaftstempel* (the Temple of Friendship) and the *Philosophenhaus* (the Philosopher's House) are both Classical in conception, while the *Speisesaal* (the Banqueting Hall), built in 1799–1802 for festive occasions, is of a unique design with concave interior walls. Four niches between the twelve French doors are painted with river scenes, and the cupola in the ceiling is decorated to resemble the sky.

*Baden, Austria*

## THE ORANGERY AT WEIKERSDORF

5

The hot springs at Baden, some eighteen miles south of Vienna, have been famous since Antiquity. To the Romans, it was simply *Aquae* (the Waters), and the legionnaires came here convinced that their wounds would heal more quickly in the hot sulfurous waters. One of the springs is still known as the *Römerquelle* (the Roman Spring).

The world of music is also indebted to Baden. It was here that Mozart, shortly before his death, composed the *Ave Verum* when visiting his wife, Constanze, who was taking the waters, while Beethoven spent fifteen summers in Baden, seeking a cure for his deafness, and wrote his *Missa Solemnis* and part of the Ninth Symphony here. Salieri, Schubert, and Johann Strauss were also regular visitors, as were many other composers and artists.

From 1813 to 1834, the Imperial Court made Baden its summer residence, and Emperor Franz I of Austria, the father-in-law of Napoleon, spent thirty-one successive summers here. (The Emperor was an enthusiastic musician who played the violin, but he was not always appreciated as an accompanist.) Prince von Metternich built a house at Baden to be near

his sovereign, and Marie Louise, Napoleon's wife, summered here with their son, the Duke of Reichstadt, known as the *Aiglon*, the Eaglet. In 1812, a devastating fire swept through

Baden, destroying nearly two-thirds of the town. It was rebuilt in a modified, somewhat understated Empire style, and today Baden has the appearance of an informal, almost cozy village.

The Orangery in the Weikersdorf park, shorn of its mansard roof and long glass wings in 1866, has been beautifully restored. It is now used for concerts and outdoor entertainments.

*Bad Homburg, Germany*

## THE BRUNNEN MONUMENT
6

## THE RUSSIAN CHURCH
7

## THE THAI PAVILION
8

Bad Homburg is a tranquil spa in the foothills of the Taunus Mountains and a favorite retreat for residents of nearby Frankfurt. Established in 1841 as the first spa in Europe with a casino, it is famous as the spot where—in the early 1890s—the Prince of Wales (later to become Edward VII) took his felt hat, dented the crown, turned up the brim, and created the homburg.

Bad Homburg was the summer residence first of the Landgraves of Hesse-Homburg from 1680 to 1866, then, from 1866 to 1918, of the Kings of Prussia (who became the Emperors of Germany in 1871). The White Tower, a relic from feudal times, overlooks the Palace and the Orangeries. Shown here are some of the colorful, smaller buildings in the spa park.

6

7

# The New Residence

## THE GARDEN PAVILION
9

## THE STATE ROOM
10

The Bamberg Castle, better known as the New Residence, was the creation of Prince-Bishop Lothar Franz von Schönborn. It is a long, rambling, asymmetrical building of rather austere appearance, but its forty-seven exquisitely appointed rooms and galleries contain one of Germany's greatest collections of historical furnishings. Shown here is one of the State Rooms.

Lothar Franz von Schonborn belonged to a prominent family, which counted among its members several Electors. They were also known as passionate builders, and many of Germany's castles and palaces owe their existence to them. This could well be the reason why Lothar Franz, when elected in 1693 to the Prince-Bishopric of Bamberg, made the solemn promise "not to build palaces or undertake costly repairs." Two years later, however, the Pope freed him from this promise and construction of the Bamberg Castle was begun. The architect was Leonhard Dientzenhofer. The Prince-Bishop took a close interest in the progress of the work and is thought to have been responsible for the grandiose design of the staircase (which was the work of Leonhard's brother, Johann). This feature how-

9

ever, could not be fitted into the castle, but was eventually used at another residence in Pommersfelden. The Garden Pavilion, also shown here, was added in 1757. Its charming Late Rococo design is ascribed to Michael Kuchels, while the garden was laid out by Balthasar Neumann.

10

*Bayreuth, Germany*

## THE NEW PALACE

*11   12*

## THE GARDEN PAVILION

*13*

Margravine Wilhelmine of Brandenburg-Bayreuth, the sister of Friedrich II of Prussia, had one of the most cultivated minds of the eighteenth century. She was a writer, composer, and architect, as well as a talented artist. The Margrave Opera House in Bayreuth is a tribute to her taste. Commissioned in 1745, it is a Baroque court theater unequaled in all of Germany and, perhaps, anywhere else. Its interiors, decorated by the Italians Giuseppe and Carlo Galli da Bibiena, are exceptional in both their richness and detail.

To the north of Bayreuth, in a charming garden setting, are two palaces. The Old Palace was built by Georg Wilhelm, as a country retreat in the form of a Carthusian monastery, where he and the members of his court could experience the simple life of monks. When his successor, Friedrich, who was Wilhelmine's husband, presented the palace to her in 1735, she set out to change its austere interior, then added two short wings and, right beside it, the New Palace. This is a graceful building consisting of two curved wings which frame the Temple of the Sun, and its exterior is

*12*

*11*

rich with incrustations of glass and pebbles. It fronts a small pond surrounded by mythological sculptures.

In the garden can be found the Roman Theater for open-air performances; an impressive Lower Grotto, dating from the 1740s and awash with nymphs and creatures from the deep; as well as a Garden Pavilion used for tea and light refreshments. A touching note is a monument to Folichon, Wilhelmine's favorite dog.

# Charlottenburg

### THE DOME OF THE CHARLOTTENBURG PALACE
*14*

### THE BELVEDERE
*15*

Charlottenburg was the first garden in Germany laid out in the French Baroque style. It was built for Sophie Charlotte, the wife of Friedrich I of Prussia in 1701. As was noted at the time, the two made an ideal couple—he had the means, while she had the taste and intelligence. (She was the daughter of the Electress Sophie of Hanover who had laid out the famous gardens at Herrenhausen.) Sophie spoke four languages, was proficient at the harpsichord, and took a keen interest in the intellectual life of Berlin. She was a good friend of the philosopher Gottfried Wilhelm Leibniz—as her mother had been before her—and appointed him president of the newly founded Academy of Science in Berlin in 1700. Much beloved and admired as the "Philosopher Queen," she died tragically from a throat infection at the age of thirty-six.

The palace garden, while laid out in the French style, shows a Dutch influence, with water serving as an important element. This was a happy choice, since the river Spree bounds it

14

on two sides. The garden contains three outstanding buildings: the Belvedere, a Baroque teahouse facing the river, built in 1788 by Carl Gotthard Langhans, the designer of the Brandenburg Gate; the Mausoleum, erected in 1810 by Karl Friedrich Schinkel to the design of Friedrich Wilhelm III for his Queen Luise; and the New Pavilion, an elegant, little Neo-Classical villa built in 1824–25, also by Schinkel, which was to become Friedrich Wilhelm III's favorite residence. Its design was borrowed from that of a villa in Naples where the King had stayed in 1822.

The Charlottenburg Palace itself is an immense structure of many periods and reflects the work of many architects; yet it forms a harmonious ensemble. The golden figure that crowns the central dome and serves as a weather vane is of the Goddess of Fortune. It dates from 1957 and replaced the original figure designed by Johann Friedrich Eosander von Göthe, which did not survive World War II.

15

## Peacock Island

### THE RUINED PALACE

*16*

Virtually untouched by the twentieth century, Peacock Island, a 200-acre nature reserve with rolling meadows, trees, shrubs, and flowers, is a mere thirteen miles from the center of Berlin. It has managed to retain its pastoral magic thanks to the protection of the German government.

The island was acquired by Friedrich Wilhelm II in 1793 from a Potsdam orphanage as a hideaway for himself and his mistress (a trumpeter's daughter named Wilhelmine Encke, whom he later ennobled as the Countess of Lichtenau). Unfortunately, he was given little time to enjoy his romantic retreat, since—only a few years later—he was knocked senseless by a flying champagne cork, and died.

His son and heir, Friedrich Wilhelm III, had more sedate ideas concerning the island and its uses. He had it landscaped into a park on the English model with oak trees and peacocks, as well as grazing sheep and cattle. He also built a dairy, and later, he added a zoo with lions and other exotic animals that eventually was to form the basis for Berlin's famous Tiergarten.

*16*

Friedrich Wilhelm III also built a number of follies on the island. Some of these have survived, although the immense Palm House was burned to the ground in 1880. One of the follies still standing is the Neo-Gothic Ruined Palace, a faux-ruin in wood, erected by a local carpenter. It has a bright, white imitation-brick center, flanked by two towers connected by an aerial bridge, and a gate painted with a landscape to look like an open gateway into the park beyond. According to contemporary sources, it was meant to represent "an old decayed Roman country seat." The interiors are an excellent example of the Neo-Classical style of the eigh-teenth century, with a touch of the exotic in the form of a Tahitian Room, whose walls and ceiling are painted to simulate a bamboo hut.

Other follies on the island include the Cavalier House of 1803 (modified in 1824–26 by Karl Friedrich Schinkel, who gave it a Late Gothic appearance by adding fragments of a fifteenth-century façade from a dismantled house in Danzig to the front of the southern tower); the Swiss House, also by Schinkel; the Hunting Hut, completely dressed in bark; the Winter House of 1828, adapted for exotic birds; the Frigate Shed of 1833, built to hold a small frigate presented to Friedrich Wilhelm III by the English court; as well as five or six others.

Friedrich Wilhelm III's son, Prince Wilhelm, "later to become something of a peacock himself" as Kaiser Wilhelm I of a united Germany, went into hiding on Peacock Island during the 1848 revolution before fleeing to England. At the height of the Nazi regime, Joseph Goebbels staged an extravaganza on the island during the 1936 Olympic Games in Berlin—the only person ever to have violated its protected status.

*Braunschweig, Germany*

## SCHLOSS RICHMOND

17  18

Schloss Richmond (the Richmond Palace) was commissioned in 1768 by Carl Wilhelm Ferdinand, hereditary Prince and later Duke of Brunswick-Wolfenbüttel, as a present to his English-born wife, Duchess Augusta, the sister of George III. It was built by the ducal architect Karl Christoph Wilhelm Fleicher and clearly shows, in its almost severe lines, the transition from Late Baroque to Classical Revival. The interiors are elaborate and have been well preserved.

To remind her of her native country, the Duchess named her new home Richmond, and engaged Capability Brown, the noted English landscape architect, to lay out the park so as "to create a Little England." But she was not to end her days there. In 1806, Carl Wilhelm Ferdinand was killed in the battle at Jena, and when the French troops occupied Brunswick Augusta fled to England, never to return.

18

*Bruchsal, Germany*

## THE ENTRANCE LODGE
*19*

The Bruchsal Palace, with its imposing Damien Tower, straddles the highway leading north to Heidelberg.

It is a large complex of more than fifty buildings erected at the height of the Baroque period, in the years between 1720–40. The builder was Cardinal Hugo Damian von Schönborn who, in addition to his high religious office, was the Elector of large areas in this part of Germany. He was a brilliant man and a passionate builder, but not necessarily easy to work with, and it required a succession of architects to complete the work. One of these, Baron von Ritter zu Grunstein, is said to have departed in a rage the day the Cardinal decided to add an extra story to the three-story Corps de Logis under construction. It fell to Balthasar Neumann, the foremost Baroque architect of the period, to complete the palace.

The construction is of brick painted in strong shades of pink, yellow, and white. The main building, the Corps de Logis, with its semicircular staircase, grotto, and richly ornamented rooms, is considered to be a gem of German Baroque architecture. It was heavily damaged during World War II, but has been meticulously restored. Shown here is the Entrance Lodge with its unusual shape, central archway, and picturesque windows.

## SCHLOSS AUGUSTUSBURG
*20*

Schloss Augustusburg (the Augustusburg Palace) at Brühl was commissioned by Clemens August, Archbishop and Elector of Cologne, to serve as his summer residence. The architect, Johann Conrad Schlaun, began construction in 1725 but due to extensive changes made by the Archbishop's court architect, François Cuvilliés, it was only completed forty years later by Clemens August's successor. It consists of three wings. In 1748–50, the western wing was provided with a splendid staircase and State Rooms designed by Balthasar Neumann.

Work on the garden was begun in 1728 to a design by Dominique Girard. In its eastern part stood two delightful wooden pavilions, the Indian House, built in 1753, and the Snail House, built in 1768. Unfortunately, both had to be pulled down, the former around 1776, the latter in 1822. A wooden figure of a Chinese dignitary from the Indian House is now preserved in the vestibule of the palace, together with the original paintings of the two buildings.

*20*

*Brühl, Germany*

## SCHLOSS FALKENLUST
21  22  23

Clemens August, the Elector of Cologne, had a passion for hunting, whether at his estate at Clemenswerth to the north or at Brühl, south of Cologne. At Brühl the prey were herons, and he placed his hunting lodge, Falkenlust, directly in the flight path between the birds' nesting grounds at Augustusburg and the Rhine river.

He built Falkenlust in 1729–40 to the designs of Cuvilliés, the noted architect he "borrowed" from his Wittelsbach relations. In terms of sheer elegance—and cost—it has few equals in German Rococo architecture. Enclosed by a handsome wrought-iron fence, the strictly symmetrical, rather sober exterior, two stories high, is finished in white stucco embellished with motifs from

the art of falconry, and crowned with a mansard roof. A widow's walk allowed the ladies to follow sedately the progress of the hunt.

The interior arrangements of the two floors are more or less identical. Each has a vestibule, salon, bedroom, and cabinets. Common to all is their

extravagant finish—scenes from falconry dominate the decor throughout. Particularly handsome are the Lacquer Cabinet with Joseph Vivien's portrait of Clemens August; the Mirror Cabinet with its gilt wood carvings; and the staircase sheathed from top to bottom in blue-and-white Dutch tiles made especially for Falkenlust by the Rotterdam workshop of Jan Aalmis.

As a true *maison de plaisance*, Falkenlust served as a meeting place for secret political talks and—so it has been said—for equally secret trysts with beautiful ladies.

Just outside the gates is the small chapel modeled after Clemens August's father Max Emanuel's Magdalenenklause at Nymphenburg. The grotto setting with shell incrustations on the walls reflects the eighteenth-century fascination with nature and the melancholy life of the hermit.

22

23

*Büdingen, Germany*

## THE LUSTHAUS
24

## THE WILD MAN
25

The Büdingen Palace reflects all the different architectural styles known since its founding as a twelfth-century stronghold. Located on the plains northeast of Frankfurt, it is one of the few Stauffen fortresses still inhabited and—quite remarkable for its 800-year history—it is still owned and occupied by the same family, the Princes Ysenburg.

The various buildings are laid out to form a many-sided enclosure for an inner courtyard, with their age decreasing from the twelfth to the seventeenth century in a clockwise direction starting from the entrance gate. Two statues of the Wild Man in front of the buildings appear to guard the entrance.

A few miles south of Büdingen, near the picturesque village of Altenhass-lau, stands a handsome pavilion, or *Lusthaus*, in a large fenced-in garden. It was built in 1806 by Heinrich Christoph Jussow, the well-known Kassel architect. It predates the Temple he erected in the Wilhelmshöhe Park, but is in the same Romantic-Classical style, with a Chinese-inspired roof. (After years of neglect, it was beautifully restored in 1989.) Among its prominent visitors have been Jacob Grimm of Grimms' Tales and Baron Elie de Rothschild.

25

24

*Dresden, Germany*

## THE GARDENS AT GROSSEDLITZ

Grossedlitz, near Dresden, was the greatest of the French formal gardens in Saxony. When the terrain was originally purchased by Count Wackerbarth in 1719 to be laid out as a garden, several buildings were erected—including the Upper Orangery that still survives. Later, in 1723, the property was bought by August II and redesigned as a Baroque garden patterned on Versailles, with formal pools and flower beds in front of a small country house giving way to broad, descending terraces. Of the King's ambitious plans for a palace complex, little was actually built, and nothing remains in its original form.

The garden still contains a number of features of great beauty, notably the *Stille Musik* (the Calm Music), a fountain surrounded by stairs adorned with putti. It was probably designed by Matthäus Daniel Pöppelmann.

*Dresden, Germany*

## THE ZWINGER
27  28  29  30

The Zwinger is a Baroque masterpiece and the pride of Dresden. As its name indicates, it is a large, outer courtyard, fronting a Rococo palace and surrounded by galleries that link seven elaborate pavilions. It was commissioned by Augustus II, the Strong, Elector of Saxony and King of Poland, designed by Matthäus Daniel Pöppelmann, and completed in 1732. The courtyard was laid out as a French garden with all its attendant features, and it was to serve the Elector as a setting for the lavish court festivities for which he was well known —a sort of open-air banqueting hall. In fact, even long before it was given its final form, and with some of the pavilions still in wood, it was the scene of the marriage of Augustus's son.

Outstanding among the pavilions are the Crown Gate, its onion dome topped by Augustus's Polish crown, and the Wall Pavilion with its satyr sculptures. Originally, they served to

27

protect the exotic plants through the winter but soon became a home for Augustus's various collections, in particular those related to natural sciences. In time, the Zwinger became the most important museum in Europe in this field.

Beside his enormous strength, Augustus had other qualities. Thomas Carlyle, the Scottish historian, described him as "The Ever-Cheerful Man of Sin." He kept a harem and left 354 illegitimate children, but he apparently found it difficult to keep track of his extended family—at least one of his daughters wound up as his mistress.

28

30

29

*Düsseldorf, Germany*

## SCHLOSS BENRATH

31

Schloss Benrath (the Benrath Palace), six miles southeast of Düsseldorf, was commissioned by the Elector Karl Theodor of Pfalz-Sulzbach and built by Nicolas de Pigage, his court architect and garden designer. It was to serve as a hunting lodge, but it soon became one of Karl Theodor's residences, perhaps following the example of Friedrich II's use of Sans Souci, a garden palace, as his official residence.

The main building, an exceptionally handsome Baroque structure, was completed in 1769. Its interior is a classic example of the French idea of "distribution" or maximum utilization of space, containing no less than eighty rooms in a shell that, from the outside, looks one and a half stories tall! Most of the rooms are barely large enough to hold a bed, but the entrance, two State Rooms, and the domed central room are spacious, as are the electoral apartments. Their original Rococo decoration shows a restraint more typical of the formal Classical style. To conserve space during entertainments, the musicians were placed between the two shells of the dome.

## SCHLOSS DYCK AND THE BRIDGE PAVILION
32

Like Münsterland to the east, the region west of the Rhine, near the Dutch border, has its *Wasserburgen*, or water-surrounded castles. Prominent among them is Schloss Dyck (the Dyck Palace), which originated as an eleventh-century fortification, was destroyed and then rebuilt, standing today as a handsome Baroque Palace, surrounded by outbuildings and protected by moats. It houses a well-known armory and an outstanding collection of Chinese silk hangings ordered by Empress Maria Theresa of Austria and depicting commercial life in China in the eighteenth century. The property has been in the same family almost since its original construction. One of its fifteenth-century ancestors is said to have been a successful *Raubritter*, or robber baron.

The park was one of the notable gardens of the nineteenth century, containing a great variety of trees and plants collected by the then-owner, Count Joseph zu Salm-Reifferscheidt Dyck. Baron von Humboldt was a visitor, and Pierre Joseph Redouté often came to paint here. His most famous watercolor of lilies hangs in the palace library. The single garden building in the foreground, the Bridge Pavilion, was built in 1769.

## THE LIECHTENSTEIN PAVILION

33

The Liechtensteins took their name from the Castle of Liechtenstein in Schellenberg, near Vienna, where the founder of the house, Hugo, lived in the twelfth century. It is now in a ruinous state, and all that remains of their property in nearby Guntramsdorf is this exquisite garden pavilion built for Prince Hartmann von Liechtenstein about 1711, possibly by Johann Lucas von Hildebrandt. The interior is decorated with grotesque frescoes with Chinese motifs.

In Mödling, also in the Vienna woods, is the Classical Temple of the Hussars of 1812, a memorial to seven soldiers who fought for the Prince of Liechtenstein at the battle of Aspern. It is concealed high up in the woods and is difficult to find. Franz Schubert once spent the night lost and alone in the area, unable to find his way home.

The Liechtensteins built two elaborate palaces in Vienna itself. The Town Palace of 1705, still owned by the reigning Prince of Liechtenstein, has a series of Rococo reception rooms, one of which has a chimney piece by Canova. The Garden Palace of 1711 is a vast Baroque structure, which now houses the Museum of Modern Art.

When the Habsburg Empire crumbled in 1918 and a large part of their property in Bohemia was lost, the Princes of Liechtenstein retired to their Medieval stronghold in Vaduz and joined their economy to that of Switzerland. Although the castle there has well over 100 rooms, there is still not sufficient space to properly display all of their famous art collections, so a museum has been established in the town of Vaduz itself, where the best pieces are shown in rotation.

33

# Herrenhausen

Herrenhausen had been the summer residence of the Dukes and later Electors of Hanover since 1666. The castle was entirely destroyed during World War II, but the garden and a number of smaller buildings either survived or have since been restored.

The celebrated Baroque Formal Garden (the *Grosser Garten*) was created by Princess Sophie, the wife of Elector Ernest Augustus. (As a Stuart, she was the granddaughter of one King of England, James I, and the mother of another, George I.) The architect was a disciple of André Le Nôtre. and it is quite possible that the great man himself had a hand in the plans.

The garden consists of a large rectangular parterre, adorned with thirty-two statuary pieces and surrounded on three sides by canals. At one end there are a number of small garden

34

segments, each with a different design and separated by hedges; and on either side of the parterre, there is a maze and a hedge theater. A powerful fountain jets its water 270 feet in the air.

The hedge theater (the *Georgsgarten Theater*) is perhaps the most important feature of Herrenhausen. It dates from 1689 and is the oldest preserved theater of its kind. The stage, delineated by clipped beech hedges, is in the shape of a trapezium and displays the well-known gilded lead statues of the ducal family in heroic poses, while

the auditorium is in the shape of an amphitheater. It is still used for outdoor performances in the summer.

The gallery, originally intended to be the Orangery, was the only castle building to survive World War II. Built in 1694, it contains a large hall

*Hanover • continued*

with music galleries and elegant frescoes. It became the favorite retreat of Sophie, who was an enthusiastic patron of the arts. (On one occasion, she commissioned a set of Gobelin tapestries depicting the life of her mother, the "Winter Queen" of Bohemia.)

35

36

37

Two pavilions at the southwest and southeast corners of the garden, built in 1705, were originally constructed of wood but, after a fire, one was rebuilt in stone.

The classical Leibniz Temple in the nearby *Berggarten* (adjacent to the *Grosser Garten*) contains a marble bust of the philosopher, who was also the court librarian.

38

39

## THE GOLDEN ROOF
*40*

The Golden Roof is an oriel or porch roofed with gilded copper tiles added to a nondescript building in Innsbruck (then the Ducal Palace), in 1494–96. Legend has it that it was created by the building's owner, Friedrich the Penniless, Duke of Styria, who, tiring of the jokes about his poverty, had the roof—which was in full view of passers-by—covered with gold coins. In reality, this charming Late Gothic structure was built to celebrate Emperor Maximilian I's marriage to Bianca Maria Sforza, his second wife, and served as a box from which the court watched the festivities in the square below. Its decoration, growing richer as it rises toward the roof, heralds the coming of the Renaissance.

The oriel has two floors. The balustrade of the lower floor is adorned with a frieze of delicately carved coats of arms of the then-rulers of Europe, while the lavishly decorated upper floor displays carvings of the Emperor and his two wives, Marie of Burgundy and Bianca Maria Sforza.

*40*

# Karlsaue

### THE MARBLE TEMPLE

*41*

This large public park stretching through the center of Kassel, is one of the oldest garden sites in Germany. In 1568, Landgrave Wilhelm IV established his palace garden here, connecting it to his residence with a bridge across the river Fulda. It was first expanded into a huge formal garden by Landgrave Karl of Hesse in the early 1700s, and then, later in the century, it was converted into a Baroque landscape garden.

Landgrave Karl's design included several garden structures that are still standing. The Orangery, completed in 1711, consists of a two-storied, central pavilion with lateral wings and two smaller buildings at either end, which served as living quarters for the Landgrave and his wife in the summer. The Orangery is flanked by two pavilions. One of these, the Marble Pavilion, built in 1728, contains a remarkable collection of Roman Baroque sculpture.

On the park's Swan Island stands a domed Marble Temple of a rather odd design. It is thought to be a nineteenth-century imitation of an eighteenth-century predecessor. Overlooking the park is a Breakfast Pavilion built in 1805 for the Elector Wilhelm I.

Today, Karlsaue plays host to any number of cultural activities, including the Documenta, an exhibit of contemporary art that takes place every four years.

*41*

*Kassel, Germany*

*Wilhelmshöhe*

THE HERCULES
MONUMENT
*42*

THE PALM HOUSE
*43*

Silhouetted sharply against the sky stands the Hercules monument on the wooded slopes of the Habicht Forest, a landmark both for Kassel and for Wilhelmshöhe Park.

It was during his travels in Italy at the turn of the seventeenth century that Landgrave Karl of Hesse was inspired to return home and create Wilhelmshöhe, which became one of the great feats of landscape planning of that era. He engaged the Italian architect Giovanni Francesco Guerniero to draw up the plans, which were published in 1706. Of the monumental designs, two-thirds were never realized, but those that were are almost overwhelming, with their central palace, temples, tombs, statues, imitation grottos, and the great waterfall cascading down 700 feet from the base of the Hercules monument. Hercules itself, modeled on the Farnese

*43*

statue in the Naples Museum, is thirty feet high. With its pedestal, the octagonal Castle of the Giants topped by a pyramid, the monument stands 233 feet high.

The park was greatly altered in the 1760s, during the reign of Friedrich II, with the addition of fountains,

lakes, canals, and bridges in the English style, together with a number of follies. Among those still standing are the Palm House, the Jussow Temple by a fountain lake, and the Lion's Castle.

# Wilhelmstal

44

45

46

The Wilhelmstal Palace was designed by the distinguished Baroque architect François Cuvilliés in 1743 as a summer residence for Landgrave Wilhelm III, but it was only completed thirty years later under his successor, Friedrich II. The interiors display a refined elegance, with carved oak paneling and—according to the taste of German princes at the time—a gallery filled with portraits of beautiful women. These were ladies (noble and not so noble) painted by the noted German artist Johann Heinrich Tischbein the Elder. One of the portraits is of the English Princess Mary, who was married to one of the young counts.

During the brief reign of Jerome, Napoleon's brother, as King of Westphalia (from 1807 to 1813), Kassel served as his capital, and he used Wilhelmstal as his residence. The decorations and furnishings in the Empire-style rooms were chosen by him.

The park was also designed by Cuvilliés, but his plans were never fully realized. The Grotto, with its shell interior, was long neglected, but it has now been fully restored with statues by Willem Rottermund, Asmis Frauen, and Jacob Cressant lining the long, reflecting pool. There is also a tower, as well as two handsome guardhouses by Simon Louis du Ry at the entrance to the park.

*Kleinglienicke, Germany*

## THE ROTUNDA
*47*

The pleasure grounds of Kleinglien-icke, stretching down to the river Havel, were created in 1816 by Peter Joseph Lenné, while he was still a gardener's assistant. They were considerably enlarged in 1822, when the park was extended in the direction of Potsdam. At that time, Karl Friedrich Schinkel created a number of garden features for Prince Karl August of Prussia—including a casino, a temple, a wrought-iron bridge, and the Rotunda. He also converted a number of already existing buildings in an Italianate style. Near the entrance to the park, the fountain, with its golden lions on high white pedestals spurting water into a shallow basin, is an exact copy of one at the Villa Medici in Rome.

The Rotunda sits at one end of the bridge that spans the Havel. Before the reunification of Germany, this river formed the demarcation line between West and East Germany, and during the Cold War era the bridge became famous as the site of the first spy-swap, when Gary Powers, the American U-2 pilot, was exchanged for the Russian agent, Rudolf Ivanovich Abel.

47

## *The Abbey*

### THE TURKISH MOSQUE
*48*

### THE FISH POND
*49  50*

Kremsmünster Abbey rises between the Danube and the foothills of the Alps. It was founded in the second half of the eighth century by Tassilo III, Duke of Bavaria, in memory of his son Gunther, who was killed by a wild boar while hunting in the domanial forests. The present appearances of most of the buildings date back to the seventeenth and eighteenth centuries.

The Turkish Mosque, for example, was constructed in 1640–42 for Abbot Bonifaz Negele. It has an elegant loggia with interior stuccos.

Among the unusual features of the Abbey is the Fish Pond built in 1691 by Carlo Antonio Carlone. The Arcades Grotto, with its statuary, its series of rough stone incrustations, five basins, and jets of water, was originally part of a complex including a pleasure pavilion built onto the lake. (This no longer exists.)

*48*

*49*

*50*

*Kulmbach, Germany*

# Sanspareil

## THE ROCK GARDEN
51

The Sanspareil Rock Garden at the foot of the Zwernitz Castle near Kulmbach is a most important monument in the history of German gardens. It is the first sentimental landscape garden on the Continent, obviously inspired by English and probably also by Italian gardens of the sixteenth century. It was created for Margravine Wilhelmine von Bayreuth in 1748, but differs totally in character from Wilhelmine's other landscape garden, the classical Hermitage at Bayreuth.

The site is a rocky grove of huge outcrops, where beech trees share the ground with isolated boulders of strange shapes. It was from this wild and romantic setting that Wilhelmine drew the inspiration for a garden design based on *Les Aventures de Télémaque*, the famous novel by Fénelon, published in 1699. In her imagination, the center of the grove was the magical island of Ogygia on which Télémaque was shipwrecked during his search for his father Odysseus. The theme of the son's selflessness was intended to inspire the hearts and minds of the visitors.

The garden was laid out by Joseph Saint-Pierre and included grottos, sculptures, and a number of garden buildings—most of which have disappeared. The rustic *Hainbau* (the Oriental House) has survived, as has a small open courtyard. (It was built around an old beech tree, which is no longer there.) There is also a Theater built as a ruin and set in a grotto, handsomely decorated with medallions, masks, and a herm.

51

## THE GREEN PAVILION

*52*

Since the thirteenth century, Laxenburg has been one of the favorite hunting grounds of Austrian rulers. Situated a mere ten miles from the center of Vienna, Laxenburg is a large park with natural planting and winding paths that is criss-crossed by streamlets, canals, and ponds. The buildings on the grounds include a rather indifferent-looking palace built in 1752, a moated Medieval castle, and a plethora of garden pavilions and follies. Laxenburg was the scene of glittering festivities during the Congress of Vienna in 1815, and it was here that Karl I, the last Austrian Emperor, met with his brother-in-law, Prince Sextus Bourbon-Parma in 1917 during World War I, to discuss possible terms for peace.

The war against the Turks in the seventeenth century played havoc with the Viennese countryside, and Laxenburg was not spared. It was only when the Ottomans had been defeated in 1683, that the gardens could be laid out again in the grand manner. Of the formal garden created at Laxenburg under Maria Theresa, a delightful, trellis-work pavilion, known as the Temple of Diana or the Green Pavilion, built in 1753, is still standing. It is in the center of the radial hunting *allées* and has a most unusual design with intricate detailing and an impressive frescoed dome. Among the later structures, there is a Classical

*52*

temple, the Concordia, built in 1795, and a number of interesting bridges and statuary. On an island in the Great Pond stands the Neo-Gothic Franzensburg, a fantasy of turrets, dungeons, and grottos. It was begun in 1798 by Franz II, Maria Theresa's grandson, in imitation of the Habsburg castle in Switzerland, and completed in 1836 when Ferdinand I ruled. It now serves as a museum.

Laxenburg was badly damaged during World War II, but it has since been restored.

*Linderhof, Germany*

## SCHLOSS LINDERHOF
53

## THE GROTTO
54

## THE FOUNTAIN
55

Of all "Mad" King Ludwig II's extravagances, Schloss Linderhof (the Linderhof Palace) was the most costly. It is also the one with the most elegant interiors and, to complete the superlatives, the one located in the most unlikely of places, deep in the forest in a remote valley of the Ammergau Alps, where Ludwig's father originally had a hunting lodge. It is also said to have been Ludwig's favorite retreat. He drew his inspiration from Versailles, which he had visited, and his obsession with the Sun King is reflected in all aspects of Linderhof. Construction was begun in 1869 when Georg Dollmann, the King's private architect, transformed the hunting lodge into a royal Neo-Baroque Palace, parts of which—notably the luxurious State Bedroom—surpassed even the elegance of Versailles.

The park was laid out in 1880 by K. von Effner, the court gardener, in the Italian villa style, breaking the steep hill slopes with terraces linked by

54

55

elaborate staircases. There are a number of curious buildings, reflecting Ludwig's love and admiration for Richard Wagner. A huge man-made cave, the Venus Grotto, with stalactites and a lake upon which floats a gilded shell-boat (electrically lit in a variety of colors for the King's visit), was inspired by the Venusberg in Wagner's *Tannhauser*. An old Germanic dwelling, built of rough logs and with a tree growing out through the roof from the center of the interior (the *Hundingshutte*), was supposed to be the Hut or dwelling of Hunding from Act I of Wagner's *Die Walkure*. Then, perched on one of the high terraces, is the Moorish Kiosk, originally constructed for the World's Fair in Paris in 1867, with a gilded dome and four towers, housing the spectacular Peacock Throne, where Ludwig, dressed as a Turkish sultan, would smoke a hookah with young boys disguised as eunuchs.

Thanks to its remote location, Linderhof survived World War II unscathed.

## MONREPOS

Ludwigsburg, with its 452 rooms, is the largest Baroque palace in Germany and one of the few large castles that escaped damage during World War II. It was built in 1704 by Duke Eberhard Ludwig of Württemberg for his mistress Wilhelmina—supposedly to keep her away from his wife in Stuttgart. Initially designed as a hunting lodge, it was repeatedly enlarged and embellished by Eberhard Ludwig's successors and a series of architects during the next sixty years, until it attained its present shape. The exterior is of golden stone and the interiors are extravagantly decorated. The Duke's bedroom speaks volumes with its ubiquitous mirrors placed at a variety of angles, and its amorous gold figures. Hidden under the dome in the east wing is a gaming room where the Duke and his friends could gamble in seclusion.

In the park, adjacent to Ludwigsburg and opposite its north front, sits the small hunting lodge Favorite. It was built in 1715 and redecorated in 1797 by Duke Friedrich I.

Some six miles from Ludwigsburg, and overlooking a lake, is the gracious Louis XV château, Monrepos, built by Philippe de la Guêpière in the 1760s, and extended in the early nineteenth century. Although its Rococo heritage is still apparent, Monrepos was one of the first of such structures to reflect an early Neo-Classical trend. The original intention was to link the château to the lake via a series of steps and terraces, but lack of money prevented the realization of this connection.

56

## THE GARDEN PAVILION
### 57

Located on the northern shore of Lake Constance—Bodensee, to the local residents—the picturesque town of Meersburg is dominated by its two castles, one dating back to early Medieval times and the other erected in 1712 by Prince-Bishop Johann VIII Franz Schenk of Stauffenberg. Adorning the latter is a small Garden (or Tea) Pavilion in Baroque stucco. Perched on a narrow ledge overlooking the town, it has a sweeping view across the lake to the hills on the opposite side. Inside the Garden Pavilion, one decorative detail of particular interest is the great delicacy with which the ceiling is painted.

57

## THE PAVILION IN THE ABBEY'S GARDEN

58

"The Abbey sits grandly upon a hill, reigning over the Danubian valley below, pointing heavenward, unquestionably religious, yet built completely in the worldly style of the eighteenth century." This is one observer's impression of Melk, which is notable both in size and in grandeur, as it stands on a rugged promontory above the river (once the site of a Carolingian fortress). Reconstruction of the earlier Gothic building was begun in 1702 by a young and talented abbot, Berthold Dietmayr, but not completed until fifty years later by his successors.

Melk has a notable history. Among its visitors, Empress Maria Theresa praised its beauty, even though she

had to be carried up its steep slopes in a hammock, and Napoleon once made it his headquarters. The Napoleonic wars, however, were not kind to the Abbey whose all too prominent site made it an obvious target, as had been the case during the wars against the Turks centuries earlier. When the Nazis occupied Austria in 1938, they invaded the Abbey, dispossessing the monks and threatening to dissolve their order.

On the upper floor, which is reached via a spiral staircase, are two Baroque reading rooms. In the small entryway to the library are two stunning wrought-iron filigree gates, while the library itself—one of the most important rooms in any Benedictine monastery—has intarsia bookshelves with the books bound to match them, and a ceiling fresco painted by Paul Troger. In 1925, to pay for much

needed repairs, it became necessary to sell a copy of the Gutenberg Bible belonging to the Abbey, as well as a number of valuable manuscripts. Fortunately, a superb collection still remains, some 85,000 volumes and 9,200 precious manuscripts, the majority dating from the fifteenth century.

To the east of the Abbey is situated the Garden Pavilion built in 1747 to the plans of Franz Munggenast. The interior is dominated by a fresco showing the Four Continents radiating around the sun, with the Signs of the Zodiac painted above.

## VIEW OF THE SCHLOSS
*59*

## THE GUARD HOUSE
*60*

## THE SCHLOSS
*61*

## THE PHEASANTRY
*62*

The core of the Electors of Saxony's Schloss at Moritzburg near Dresden was built in 1542–46 for the Elector Moritz. It was enlarged and given its present form from 1723 onward by Pöppelmann. Many of the interiors with their rich wall hangings, wood carvings, and furnishings have been preserved in their original state.

The Pheasantry, a small hunting lodge nearby, was constructed for August III in 1769–82. It is an elegant Neo-Classical building with chinoiserie touches, such as the Chinese figures on the roof.

Down by the lake is a charming folly, a miniature harbor with a toy lighthouse, built in 1780.

*59*

*60*

*61*

*62*

## The Hofgarten

### THE GARDEN BUILDING

63

One of the finest German Renaissance gardens to have survived is the Hofgarten, the island garden of the Residenz Palace in Munich, laid out in 1613. It is centered around the Garden Building, a fountain pavilion in the form of a twelve-sided temple to Diana topped by a bronze figure of the goddess (1594), later converted into an allegorical statue of Bavaria.

Paths radiate out from this pavilion in every direction. The garden itself has been replanted with chestnut trees, flowerbeds, and fountains as specified in the original seventeenth-century plan, and is almost entirely enclosed by long arcades, 2,000 feet in length. These arcades are decorated with historical frescoes, and lined with art galleries and cafés.

63

# Nymphenburg

One of the architectural favorites of Ludwig II was the Amalienburg, the fourth pavilion at Nymphenburg. It was built in 1739 by François Cuvilliés, the dwarf whose astonishing career escalated from court jester to great architect. (The Elector Max Emanuel was so fond of him that, on one occasion, Cuvilliés was hidden in a birthday pie to be served as a surprise at the royal table.)

Long considered one of the triumphs of German Rococo, the Amalienburg was built as a gift for Amalia, the wife of Max Emanuel's son, Karl Albrecht. Amalia felt she was the embodiment of Diana, the goddess of the chase, and the Hunting Room reflects this feeling. Despite this conviction, however, she preferred to observe the hunt with her ladies-in-waiting from the circular balcony that crowns the

64

65

66

67

building. The pavilion's silvered halls provided the dazzling setting for regal parties—masked balls and Venetian galas with gondoliers plying the canals—while its kitchen, lined with Delft tiles, was the perfect stage for make-believe toil.

Early in the nineteenth century, Ludwig I visited Amalienburg with his courtesan, Lola Montez. His son, Ludwig II, reveled in the pavilion, particularly in the candlelight images of himself reflected in the silver and blue Hall of Mirrors. Richard Wagner, visiting the pavilion as the guest of Ludwig II, exclaimed: "Nothing, anywhere, could be more charming!"

68

Nymphenburg was the summer residence of the Electors of Bavaria. It consists of a central Palace, the Nymphenburg Schloss, designed by Agostino Barelli and Enrico Zuccalli, and built in the Italian style toward the end of the seventeenth century, and four Baroque pavilions set in a large park with formal gardens, lakes, and crisscrossed by canals. (See above for a description of Ludwig II's favorite, the Amalienburg.)

Josef Effner, a gardener's son, born in nearby Dachau and trained in Paris, was the architect responsible for the other three pavilions: the Pagodenburg built in 1719; the Badenburg, with its banqueting hall and a two-story bathing apartment, built in

70

69

71

1721; and the Magdalenenklause, built in 1725, and intended as a hermitage with its chapel of tufa encrusted with shells. The craftsmen who labored so diligently on these pavilions were also from Bavaria, having been chosen, for the first time, over their French and Italian counterparts. The Pagodenburg was commissioned by the Blue Elector, Max Emanuel, whose amorous excesses peopled his kingdom with illegitimate Wittelsbachs, as well as with a vast debt. In celebration of the end of a ten-year exile (following his defeat at the hands of the Duke of Marlbor-

ough at Blenheim), he had this jewel of chinoiserie built in accordance with a design he had already used for his hunting lodge near Brussels, when he served as governor of the Netherlands. Further Dutch influence is evident in the nearly two thousand faience tiles that embellish the ground floor and the walls of the staircase. Two upstairs rooms, the Black and the Red Cabinets, are lacquered with the Chinese scenes that have given the pavilion its name. The main octagonal salon is only twenty-seven feet across, so the dining table occupies most of the available space. It thus became customary for the Elector and his guests to have their dinner served to them through the windows. Of

course, when he was entertaining one of his favorite mistresses, a smaller table could be set up in one of the intimate alcoves.

In 1863, when Prince Otto von Bismarck visited the Pagodenburg, he learned that Ludwig II, then residing at the Palace, was attending lectures in physics and mathematics at Munich University. Nonetheless, in his autobiography, Bismarck deplored Ludwig's total lack of interest in any field other than the artistic.

Despite its early Italian and French geometric influence, the park was eventually given a less formal, more romantic design with natural-looking lakes and meandering pathways. A wide canal, cascading its water into the Würm canal below, is linked to the ponds and moats surrounding the main building that give the Palace the appearance of floating on water.

72

## THE STAG PAVILION
*73*

The Stag Pavilion in Munich is of relatively recent origin. It stands at the end of Nymphenburger Strasse at the entrance to the canal where the Wittelsbach royal family embarked each summer on the final leg of the journey (by barge) from the Residenz to the Nymphenburg Schloss.

73

## Schleissheim

### THE LUSTHEIM

74

The grand scale of Schleissheim's Neues Schloss (New Palace) is a reflection of the Elector Max Emanuel's excessive passion for building, a mania shared by many of his contemporaries in eighteenth-century Germany. Fortunately for his subjects, the Elector's exile in France from 1704 to 1714 prevented him from realizing certain grandiose schemes—such as the enormous corridors meant to link the Palace with the garden pavilion, or *Lustheim*, a mile or so distant. The Palace, whose façade is 1,100 feet long, was much too large to be functional and, according to Baron de Montesquieu, the French philosopher, the electoral court was actually too small to fill it.

One outstanding feature is its splendid staircase, richly decorated in stucco-work, which leads to the state apartments on the first floor.

The park was laid out by the Frenchmen Carbonet and Girard, in accordance with a French design of flowerbeds, canals, and a waterfall. The *Lustheim*, a garden pavilion designed in 1684 by Enrico Zuccalli in an Italianate style, is situated at the eastern end of the park. It contains a large, high-ceilinged salon with frescoes and fine moldings, and houses one of the world's most important collections of Meissen porcelain.

Across from the Neues Schloss stands the Altes Schloss (Old Palace), built in 1616–23. Although it was severely damaged in World War II, it has since been partly restored and partly rebuilt. It is now a branch of the Bavarian National Museum.

## *Nordkirchen Palace*

### A STATUE IN THE FORMAL GARDEN

75

The Münster region is dotted with small palaces, formerly fortifications, which trace their origin back to the Teutons. More often than not, they are located on islands or surrounded by moats, and are thus know as *Wasserburgen,* or "châteaux surrounded by water."

Of these, Nordkirchen Palace, an eighteenth-century ensemble, is often referred to as the small Versailles of Westphalia. It has an elegant Formal Garden laid out by Johann Conrad Schlaun in 1725 and redesigned by Achille Duchène in 1906. Of the

original layout, the front of the Oranienburg and Orangery in the *Westgarten* has been preserved. The palace presently serves as a school of finance.

## Ober-Siebenbrunn, Austria

### THE SUMMER HOUSE
*76    77*

The seventeenth-century Palace at Ober-Siebenbrunn (located on the Marchfeld plain east of Vienna) that once belonged to Archbishop Sigismund Kolonics, was acquired by Emperor Karl VI in 1720 and presented to Prince Eugene, who had triumphed over the Turkish forces at Belgrade.

Eugene had the Palace remodeled and the park laid out in the French style, as at Versailles. The Palace has remained comparatively unchanged since then, but the lack of water, caused by the drying up of the seven wells that had given the Palace its name, has greatly reduced the scopé of the park.

The Summer House in the park has survived intact. It was built for Prince Eugene by Johann Lucas von Hildebrandt in 1725–30 and features fine Baroque surface ornaments over its doors and windows. It is best known, however, for its grotesque ceiling frescoes picturing the Four Seasons, the Signs of the Zodiac, the Compass Points, and the Pleasures of Country Life.

*77*

*76*

THE CHINESE PAVILION

THE ENGLISH PAVILION

THE GREAT GONDOLA

Pillnitz's early history reads like a Grimms' fairy tale. It begins sometime in the Middle Ages with a moated stronghold, replaced by a castle built on its ruins in the early 1600s. The castle was then acquired by Elector Johann Georg who gave it to his mistress, Countess Sybille von Rochlitz in 1694. This displeased his wife and in the altercation that followed, the Elector tried to kill her but was prevented from doing so by his brother, "who wrested the sword from his hand." Soon after, however, both the mistress and her lover died from smallpox. The new Elector, August II, later to become King of Poland, in turn gave the castle to his mistress, Countess Anna Constanze Cosel. But this highly ambitious lady was hardly more fortunate than the previous owner—she lost favor in the eyes of her lover and fled from Pillnitz in 1715, only to be captured and incarcerated for the rest of her life.

In 1718, Elector August took possession of the castle once more and commissioned his superintendent, Count Wackerbarth, to plan a huge new castle to serve as his pleasure pavilion.

Matthaus Daniel Pöppelmann was then engaged to prepare the design, and the first result of this so-called Great Plan of 1720 was the Water Palace, one of the first buildings in Germany inspired by a fanciful Chinese style. It was connected to the river Elbe by a flight of steps adorned with two sphinxes. The steps ended at a boathouse complete with gondolas, in which the Elector would ply the river.

The next step in the Great Plan was construction of the Mountain Palace in 1722, complementing the Water Palace—to which it was linked by an elaborate parterre. This, however, was effectively the end of the Plan, since the two buildings now closed off the

79

area that was to have been covered by the overall design. The two palaces were later connected to the seventeenth-century castle, to which a Temple of Venus was added (replacing a Protestant church when the Elector converted to Catholicism in order to assume the Polish throne). In 1818, the old castle was destroyed in a fire but was rebuilt as the New Palace by C. F. Schuricht.

Among the garden structures are the Chinese Pavilion filled with chinoiserie paintings, built to a design by Sir William Chambers; the English Pavilion, a teahouse with an elegant interior, built in 1784; and an artificial castle ruin—now more ruinous than it was intended to be—that was added to the garden in 1785.

*Potsdam, Germany*

## THE PYRAMID
*81*

Potsdam emerged in the seventeenth century as the capital of the Brandenburg Principality (the fief of the Hohenzollerns), later to become part of Prussia. Since then, its history has been inextricably linked to that of Germany. It was in Potsdam that Friedrich Wilhelm I, The Soldier King, reviewed his giant grenadiers and turned Prussia into a military power. It was there that his son, Friedrich II, "The Great," built his dream palace, Sans Souci, and where he gathered together the elite of Europe's artistic and intellectual circles. It was also in Potsdam, centuries later (in 1933), that Adolf Hitler, newly elected Chancellor, received Field Marshal Paul von Hindenburg's blessing in the Garrison Church, and—at the end of World War II—the victorious Allies met in Potsdam to decide Germany's fate.

Today, Potsdam is a green and pleasant town some twenty miles to the southwest of Berlin, tucked away among verdant hills and encircled by the Havel river, as well as by small lakes. It suffered severely during

*81*

World War II, and many of its historical buildings and monuments—such as the Garrison Church with the tombs of the two Friedrichs and the old Town Palace from the seventeenth century—are gone forever. Among the more important survivors, however, are the former Orangery (later the Royal Stables), the only remaining part of the Town Palace, which now serves as the Film Museum; the Brandenburg Gate from 1770; the Military Orphanage, founded by Friedrich Wilhelm I and enlarged by his son in 1771; the Neuen Gate built in 1755 as part of the town wall; Saint Nicolas Church designed by Karl Friedrich Schinkel; and the picturesque Pumping Station (in the form of a mosque from the Arabian Nights), which supplies the water for the Sans Souci gardens. Peculiar to Potsdam is its Dutch Quarter with brightly colored, gabled houses built in 1737–40 by Johann Boumann.

To the northwest of Potsdam lies the New Park, developed by landscape gardener Johann August Eyserbeck for Friedrich II in 1786. It is a wooded area that encloses the Heiliger See on three sides and extends northward to the banks of the Havel. On the shore of the lake stands the Marble Palace, designed in the Greco-Roman style by Carl Gontard for a nephew of Friedrich II, Friedrich Wilhelm II (or "Fat Wilhelm"), of whom it was said that he was more interested in the attractiveness of his mistresses than in politics. Also on the shore is the Neo-Gothic Library, while deep in the woods stands the Alexander Nevski Chapel, an onion-crowned, Orthodox church and, next to it, a wooden chalet in the Russian style. Both were designed by P. J. Lenné in 1825 and erected by Friedrich Wilhelm III for the twelve surviving singers of the Russian Yorksche Corps who were taken prisoner during the Napoleonic wars.

Near the entrance to the park is the Orangery from 1791, decorated with antique motifs representing the Sphinx and various Egyptian gods. In a meadow nearby stands a Pyramid inscribed with hieroglyphs, which once served as an icehouse.

*Potsdam, Germany*

# Sans Souci

82

83

In 1745, when Frederick II decided to build a summer residence, a retreat to which he could withdraw from the cares of his rulership, he chose for its site a hilly vineyard near the village of Potsdam, with a sweeping view of the beautiful Havel landscape. He made Georg von Knobelsdorff his architect, and together they drew up the plans for a palace and surrounding park, assisted by the country's ablest artists and artisans. The result is Sans Souci.

Today, the 717 acres of the Sans Souci park comprise one of Europe's great pleasure gardens. Its focal point is still the Palace that gave it its name, a one-storied, rather small, but beautifully designed and ornamented building. Since its initial construction, however, a great many buildings and garden structures have been added, and the park itself has been vastly extended. Foremost among the newer buildings is the New Palace, a sprawling complex erected by Frederick II in 1763 to celebrate his victory in the Seven Years War, and which he himself referred to as rather a "show-off." In fact, he made his point by topping off the New Palace with a group of three nude statues representing the Empress, the Tsarina, and Madame de Pompadour (the wives and the mistress of his opponents in the war), holding up his crown.

Closer to the original Palace, and possibly more pleasing to the eye, are the richly ornamented Picture Gallery of 1755 (the first museum in Germany built specifically for that purpose); the Orangery of 1851, modeled on the Villa Medici in Rome and intended to serve as a winter garden and residence for high-ranking visitors; and the so-called New Chambers of 1747 which, with its large windows, was originally intended as an Orangery but was later converted to a guest house. In the park, to the south, lies Schloss Charlottenhof, an Italian villa of classic design, built for Crown Prince Friedrich Wilhelm in 1826–29 by K. F. Schinkel, and based on the Prince's own sketches.

Among the more important garden structures is the Chinese Teahouse of 1754, a splendid round green and gold pavilion, decorated with Chinese

84

85

86

figures in various poses and crowned by a mandarin with a parasol. The figures have European faces and most are dressed in Roman togas—reflecting popular ideas concerning the Middle Kingdom at the time. (The features of Voltaire, who was one of Frederick II's honored guests at Sans Souci, and his writer-in-residence for three years, can be seen on the face of one of the monkeys decorating the pavilion.)

Also to be found in the garden are the Trellis Pavilion with its golden sun emblem; the Neptune Grotto adorned with shells and topped by a statue of the sea god; the Dragon House, a Chinese-style pagoda with sixteen gilded dragons decorating its curved roof; and the Roman Baths, reminiscent of ancient Roman houses in Herculaneum, but never intended to serve as a site for actual bathing.

87

89

90

91

92

93

95

94

*Radevormwald, Germany*

## THE WOODEN PAVILION
*97*

This charming garden pavilion is one of the last well-preserved examples of rural Rococo in the Ruhr Valley. The Wooden Pavilion was built in 1772 in a timber-frame style accented with slate.

97

# Hellbrunn

98

Marcus Sitticus, Prince-Archbishop of Salzburg from 1612 to 1619, spent most of his youth in Italy. It is thus no surprise that he turned to Santino Solari, the architect of Salzburg's Cathedral, for the design of his palace and gardens at Hellbrunn. They remain largely intact today.

The stone for the buildings was quarried on the property. When all the construction had been completed, the quarry was transformed into an amphitheater whose remarkable double archway was later copied (in the 1740s) both at Sanspareil and at the Hermitage, near Bayreuth. In 1617, Hellbrunn thus became the setting for one of the first outdoor operas north of the Alps—a highlight being the performance of Monteverdi's *Orfeo*.

99

*Salzburg · continued*

Marcus Sitticus had been so intrigued by the water fantasies in the Italian gardens he had known that he ringed his palace with them in a series of grottos, alcoves, and temples. There were the Orpheus Grotto, the Mirror Grotto, the Birdsong Grotto with its trilling birds, the Crown Grotto with a metal crown that could be raised and lowered by a vertical jet of water, and the Neptune Grotto with its focus being the Big Mouth, a strange contrivance with a rolling head, whose mouth would open and fill with water. Once the lower jaw was full of water, a tongue would emerge, wagging in a very spirited fashion. This has often been viewed as Marcus Sitticus's retort to those who criticized his extravagances.

100

101

102

*103*

*104*

The most diverting of Marcus Sitticus's creations is the Sovereign's Table where his guests would be seated at a stone table with a central trough of running water to cool the wine. Whenever the company became too raucous—a not unusual occurrence in those days—a signal would be given and water would spurt out of jets concealed in the guests' seats.

A marvelously ingenious mechanical theater, powered by water, was installed at Hellbrunn in 1750. On the hill above the palace stands the One-Month Mansion, built in an astonishing thirty days to settle a wager between Marcus Sitticus and the Archduke Maximilian of Austria.

106

107

Johann Bernhard Fischer von Erlach was one of the Austrian Baroque's ablest architects, but he was also known for his hot temper. He was the Count of Schönborn's first choice to build the Schönborn Palace some thirty miles northwest of Vienna, but the two men had a falling-out and Fischer von Erlach was replaced by the more tactful Johann Lucas von Hildebrandt. Von Hildebrandt completed the Palace in 1717 and went on to receive a number of additional commissions from the Count's extended family.

Most of the original Schönborn Palace garden with its ponds, parterres, and fountains has disappeared. The two-part, half-moon Orangery with large sculptures lining the balustrades (reminiscent of Weikersheim) is in a lamentable condition. However, a shimmering pond reflects the outlines of a small Indian Temple, quite light and airy in aspect, which has been preserved.

109

After the sack of Heidelberg in 1689, the Palatine Electors turned their attentions to the royal residence at Schwetzingen. The area became a mecca for asparagus lovers, and includes a park full of surprises and delights. The architect Nicolas de Pigage is largely responsible for the garden, a basic French design with statuary, fountains, and pavilions appearing among the greenery and promenades.

The Bath House, built by the Elector Carl Theodor both for relaxation and quiet, as well as for his numerous trysts, is the outstanding architectural feature of the park and is considered one of the jewels of the German Rococo. The Temple of Botany was built to resemble the massive trunk of an oak tree, while the Grove of Apollo, with its miniature cascade, is Classical in style. The ruined Temple of Mercury and the Ruin of a Roman Waterway (from which there is an excellent view of the Rhine plain), are both early Romantic touches dotting the landscape.

110

111

The Mosque of 1780 supposedly cost 120,000 gulden, a large sum in those days, and was Carl Theodor's crowning achievement. Certainly it was much admired by the Shah of Persia in 1889 when he was a guest of the Grand Duke of Baden at Schwetzingen.

112

113

A number of artists stayed at Schwetzingen. Mozart played in the gardens as a child, and Schiller found inspiration there for his *Don Carlos*.

115

114

116

117

118

119

## CLEMENSWERTH

*120  121*

Clemenswerth, near the village of Sögel in Germany's northwest corner, is yet another retreat laid out in 1736–50 by Johann Conrad Schlaun for that passionate huntsman— Clemens August, Prince-Bishop of Münster and Paderborn. Considered one of Schlaun's most brilliant designs, it is organized in the form of a giant wheel, with the central building forming the hub and eight pavilions set in a circle around it. The central building is shaped as an octagon with four wings, forming a cross. In addition to serving as guest quarters, the Pavilions provided sufficient space for a library, a kitchen, servants' quarters, a cellar for preserving game, and stabling for a hundred horses. There was also a small Capuchin monastery with a formal yew garden sheltering a hideaway (the Gloriette) for the private use of the Prince.

Beyond the circle of pavilions and extending the "spokes" connecting them to the central building, eight straight lanes were cut through the forest, forming a star. This is the *Jagdstern* (Hunting Star) developed in the Middle Ages to facilitate hunts on horseback.

*120*

*121*

## SCHLOSS SOLITUDE

In 1763, when Duke Carl Eugen of Württemberg decided to build a new Palace in the hills between Stuttgart and Ludwigsburg, he named it "Solitude," because he had in mind a quiet place to which he could escape from Württemberg court life. However, by the time he had satisfied his passion for building on this site some eight years later, it had become any-thing but a retreat. It consisted of a central Palace—one of the finest creations of German Baroque—surrounded by extensive outbuildings in a 200-acre park filled with pavilions, fountains, ponds, and numerous statues. Today, just the core of the Palace remains. Only a few years after its construction had been completed, Carl Eugen—turning his fancy toward a new country seat, Hohen-heim—seems to have lost interest in Schloss Solitude, and it was used only on special occasions. Most of the furnishings in the outbuildings were removed or disappeared, and the gardens were more and more neglected until, eventually, little remained to suggest their past glory. Fortunately, some of Solitude is now being restored.

garden structures were the Chinese Teahouse, modeled on one at Sans Souci; the Laurel Hall, serving as an Orangery for laurel and fig trees; an island pavilion of outlandish design; and a small theater in the form of a cave covered with painted canvas depicting rocky scenes with trees and moss.

As part of the Solitude complex there was also a small castle with a boat house to accommodate a fleet of fanciful gondolas near a small body of water two miles to the south, called Bear Lake. The ducal boat was painted red with gilded carvings that highlighted the royal coat of arms supported by mermaids, two whales, and a dragon.

The death of Duke Carl Eugen in 1793 brought an end to one of the most singular and intriguing architectural experiments in palace and garden construction on record anywhere.

*123*
The Palace, designed by Philippe de la Guêpière, stands on an arcaded base and is served by magnificent, almost theatrical dual staircases. It contains a suite of extravagantly decorated rooms with superb stucco-work and inlaid floors. One of the few

pieces of original furniture remaining is a desk that belonged to Friedrich I (named King of Württemberg by Napoleon in 1806), that had been duly hollowed out to accommodate his enormous girth.

Schloss Solitude is situated on the edge of a relatively high plateau where little water is available. To supply the

garden, with its tree-lined *allées*, flowerbeds, fountains, and ponds, water had to be pumped up, using ingeniously designed machines. Little remains of the garden today—its southern parts have reverted to forest, while the rest is used for the cultivation of fruit. Among the more unusual

## THE PRATER PAVILION
*124*

The woodlands along the Danube river were documented as early as 1403. In the sixteenth century, Emperor Maximilian II established a game preserve there for the exclusive use of the Imperial Court, but in 1766 Joseph II opened the entire area —the Prater—to the public. Always a meeting place of the noble, the wealthy, and the fashionable, it became immensely popular in the 1860s, during the heyday of the Strausses and the Viennese waltz, with its many cafés devoted to singing and dancing.

Today, the Prater covers a vast area filled with swimming pools, restaurants, a race track, a stadium, a golf course and, above all, the famous amusement park with its giant Ferris wheel. At the far end of the impressive, almost three-mile straight *Hauptallee* stands the Prater Pavilion, where once the members of the imperial party would refresh themselves during the hunt. It was remodeled in 1782 by Isidor Canevale and again, in the nineteenth century, when a ceiling painting was added to its adornment. It now serves as a restaurant-café.

*124*

## Schönbrunn

125

126

In 1696, after the defeat of the Turks at the gates of Vienna, Emperor Leopold I commissioned Fischer von Erlach to create a palace and gardens that would rival Louis XIV's Versailles. The original designs were so ambitious (and the cost so enormous) that they had to be abandoned, yet the end result, with its vast park, walled avenues of clipped trees, superb sculptures, and cascades, is a majestic spectacle nonetheless.

Among the most important structures is the Gloriette, an elegant colonnade some 445 feet long and built in 1775, which occupies the site originally intended for the palace. It offers unparalleled views of Vienna and the mountains beyond.

The Menagerie, constructed of wrought iron in the shape of a star, was built for Francis I in 1752. It circles an octagonal Baroque pavilion that once housed a number of parrots. The birds are said to have come from the aviary at the Belvedere Palace. Sham ruins appeared in the park in 1778 and there are several delightful secret gardens with trellised pavilions near the palace. The exceptionally large and handsome Palm House was not added until 1883.

Schönbrunn has enchanted many famous visitors. Marie Antoinette, the daughter of Maria Theresa and Franz I, spent her childhood here. Mozart, at the age of six, performed here for the Empress Maria Theresa and, in 1786, directed his opera, *The Impresario*, at the charming little palace theater. Napoleon made it his headquarters in 1805 and 1809, when the French army occupied Vienna, and after the fall of the French Empire in 1815, his wife, Marie Louise and their son spent some of their happiest moments in exile strolling in the park.

During the Congress of Vienna in 1815, a magnificent skating party was staged for the visiting dignitaries. Handsomely decorated sleighs formed a circle around the frozen lake where European and Chinese dances were performed by skaters in exotic costumes. A young Englishman demonstrated his dual skills of skating and diplomacy by tracing on the ice the monograms of the empresses, queens, and other ladies in attendance.

128

129

130

## THE SECESSION BUILDING

*131*

At the end of the last century, a number of artists in Vienna seceded from what they considered to be the intolerably conservative art association of the establishment—the Künstlerhaus. They formed a new group, which they named "the Secession," and their motto was "To each age its art. To art its freedom."

In 1897, they had a new gallery built for them on land donated by the city administration. The architect of this Art Nouveau gem was Josef Maria Olbrich, a protégé of Otto Wagner. A 112-foot Beethoven Frieze painted by Gustav Klimt for the Beethoven Exhibition of 1902 was installed in a special basement room.

With its open-work cupola made of gilded bronze leaves, the Secession Building is a great favorite of the Viennese, who refer to it affectionately as the "Golden Cabbage."

*131*

*132*

Otto Wagner (1841–1918) was the leading architect of Vienna's Art Nouveau movement, the Secession. When the city railway was built between 1884 and 1900, he was made chief architect of the huge project, for which he drew up over two thousand plans. Although modern in feeling, the railway pavilions all harmonize well with the Baroque masterpieces around them.

The two Karlsplatz stations with their green and gold wrought-iron door grilles, and their gilded sunflowers, have become city icons. The Hof Pavilion built for the Emperor and his family has apertures reminiscent of Schönbrunn itself. Both the silk which decorated the walls of the interior and the carpeting on the floor bear the philodendron motif at the special request of the Empress Elizabeth, whose favorite plant it was. Extravagantly, this station was used only once—for the inaugural run of the railway. The conservatism of the royal household triumphed in their preference for more sedate forms of transportation. The building is now a museum.

Wagner's House or Villa and the adjoining Garden House are playful in design and Mediterranean in feeling. The Villa stands on a wooded hill with pergolas at either end, embellished with delicate wrought-iron lattice railings and intricate niches for statuary. On the façade there is a plaque inscribed with the architect's maxim, which can be translated as: "Without art, without love, there is no life."

*134*

*133*

*Waldsassen, Germany*

## THE ABBEY PAVILION

Waldsassen Abbey, located between Bayreuth and the Czech border, was founded in 1133. Accorded special privileges by the German emperors and protected by the popes, it prospered, and in 1179 a new Abbey church, built of stone, was consecrated in the presence of Friedrich Barbarossa. (This edifice stood until late in the seventeenth century.)

The introduction of the Reformation to this part of Germany in the sixteenth century led to the dissolution of the Abbey in 1560, but when the country returned to Catholicism after the Thirty Years' War, it was resettled by the Cistercians in 1661. Twenty years later, in 1681, all the old buildings were razed to be replaced by a new complex of Baroque design, completed in 1704. Then, in 1803, another dissolution took place as a result of secularization, but in 1863 a group of Cistercian nuns established a school for girls there.

The library is famous as one of the finest examples of profane Baroque art. It was completed in 1726 under the Abbot Eugen Schmid. Ten life-size wooden figures, carved by local artists, seem to support the gallery and depict the various individuals who take part in the making of a book, from the rag-gatherer providing the raw materials to the bookseller. They are both profoundly realistic and very humorous, but they exemplify—as a warning to monks and visitors alike—the pride and haughtiness that are such contrasts to the Cistercian ideal of humility.

The abbot and his monks did not always see eye to eye when it came to land ownership. At Waldsassen, an early abbot chose to protect his property with a moat (long since filled in). The pavilion shown here was one of four towers placed in the corners of the property—within the moat.

*Weikersheim, Germany*

## THE LUSTHAUS

*136*

## THE BANQUETING HALL

*137*

Since the Middle Ages, Weikersheim has been one of the ancestral seats of the Hohenlohe family. Originally a moated stronghold, it was rebuilt as a Renaissance Castle at the end of the sixteenth century. Its sumptuous Banqueting Hall dates from this period. Together with that of the Heiligenberg Castle of the Fürstenbergs, it represents one of the only two well-preserved halls from the great era of German castle building. The coffered ceiling is decorated with hunting scenes from around the world, while life-size animals, sculptured in stucco jut out from the upper walls. On either side of the monumental fireplace, painted stucco figures of Count Wolfgang and his wife, sister of William the Silent, recline as Jesse and the Virgin.

*136*

The garden, laid out in the French manner, is even more theatrical in design. At the far end, two semicircular Orangeries, running the entire length of the parterre, originally framed an equestrian statue of Count Carl Ludwig, with the vista of the Tauber valley as a backdrop. (The statue has since been removed.) Perched on the roofs of these Orangeries are a group of symbolic figures of the Seasons, the Elements, and the Regions of the World, while a touch of humor was added to the terrace balustrade in the placement of a line of grotesque dwarfs representing members of the royal household. Unfortunately, at the moment, the Orangeries are under scaffolding.

The kitchen garden includes a small pavilion, or *Lusthaus*, built in 1715, with a grotto or a bird house below and a painted room above.

*137*

*138*

*138*

In 1768, when Prince Franz of Anholt-Dessau, "The Enlightened Prince," assumed the reign of his principality, he dedicated it to Philosophy and the Liberal Arts. Breaking away from both his ancestors' military tradition and his pompous Late Baroque surroundings, he turned his eyes toward Germany's neighbors, where more enlightened trends were taking hold in many fields. Together with his close friend and advisor, the architect Friedrich Wilhelm von Erdsmannsdorff, he traveled to England and was impressed by its

*140*

advanced democracy, its industrial and agricultural reforms, as well as its informal country houses and Neo-Classical buildings. Later, while visiting Italy, he was overwhelmed by the beauty of the Roman edifices and works of art. Inspired by these experiences—and also influenced by Rousseau's works in France—he set out to create a landscape park embodying the best of the new aesthetics. The result is Wörlitz.

The park is a large, 300-acre area on the Elbe river halfway between Wörlitz and Dessau. It consists essentially of five independent gardens, separated by lakes and canals and connected by bridges and ferries. The basic layout is the result of a close cooperation between the Prince and Von Erdmannsdorff, and the plans were realized by the three gardeners, Schoch, Eyserbeck, and Neumark who, incidentally, gave their names to the gardens in their charge.

Von Erdmannsdorff was also responsible for the design and erection of practically all the structures in the park, including a palace, pavilions, follies, grottos, statues, and numerous bridges. Among the more important structures are a small Neo-Classical garden building with fine ceiling stuccos, originally referred to as "the Country House," and the Gothic House, one of the earliest Neo-Gothic buildings in Germany. It was built in 1773 as a gardener's lodging but remodeled in 1813 to serve as the Prince's residence—housing his mistress (the gardener's daughter by whom he had three children), and his art collection. Of the latter, a unique set of Swiss stained glass from the sixteenth and seventeenth centuries still remains.

*141*

*142*

*143*

Other garden structures include the English Seat, the Summer House, and the Synagogue (also known as the Vesta Temple), all located near the Palace. Overlooking the canals are the Eisenhart with its South Sea Pavilion, and the Library. The Rock is a small artificial island crowded with a Roman amphitheater, grottos, two temples, a columbarium, a miniature Vesuvius volcano that could be activated, as well as a reproduction of William Hamilton's villa on Posillipo. Even the Prince found this to be too much. Other follies are the Pantheon, the Egeria Grotto, the Flora Temple, and the Nymphaeum. Among the bridges, the Chinese or White Bridge is particularly beautiful, and on a small island by the entrance to the park, called Rousseau's Island, stands a monument to the great philosopher.

In spite of its size, Wörlitz is actually only part of the Prince's ambitious scheme to develop the land along some fifteen miles of the Elbe bank into a continuous landscape garden. This plan was never fully realized, but it would have included the now isolated gardens of Georgium and Luisium.

*Veitshöchheim*

## THE GROTTO

## THE GAZEBO

## THE CHINESE PAVILION

## THE PARNASSUS GROUP

145

146

147

About five miles downstream from Würzburg on the right bank of the river Main lies Veitshöchheim, the summer residence of the Prince-Bishops of Würzburg. It was commissioned in 1680 by Prince Philipp von Dernbach after plans by Antonio Petrini, and was enlarged and embellished in 1749 by Prince-Bishop Karl Philipp von Greifenklau, with the addition of two wings and a staircase designed by Balthasar Neumann. The interior is a happy blend of Baroque, Rococo, and Neo-Classical styles.

What makes Veitshöchheim a particular delight to visit is its park. Originally laid out as a pheasant preserve, it evolved under a succession of princes and designers, notably Balthasar Neumann and the master gardener J. Prokop Mayer, into one of Germany's most beautiful gardens and certainly the country's greatest surviving Rococo garden. With no alignment to the main building, it is not a palace garden in the classic French Baroque style, but rather a hedge garden, enclosed by high walls, with a grid of criss-crossing paths, small garden rooms, pavilions, a grotto, and a large, central pond fed by wells and emptying its waters into the Main river. There are statues everywhere (no less than 320), fronting the palace on two sides, surrounding the large pond and a smaller one, and outlining the park

*Würzburg · continued*

with Roman gods, allegories of the Arts and the Four Seasons, as well as musicians, putti, and gentlemen and ladies of the court. From the center of the large pond arises Mount Parnassus, topped by Pegasus, the winged steed, and with a built-in chime whose tones blend with that of the

cascading fountain. The statuary is by Ferdinand Tietz and Peter Wagner.

Among the garden structures, there are two circular pavilions in wood with slate roofs and delicate ceiling frescoes, ornamented Chinese follies with sandstone columns, and a grotto

148

with encrusted stones and shells, as well as sculptured dragons, lions, monkeys, and other exotic monsters. It is surmounted by an elegant, Neo-Classical pavilion with a lovely ceiling fresco, the Belvedere, built by Materno Bossi in 1772.

# BIBLIOGRAPHY

Alex, Reinhard, and Kuhn, Peter, *Schlösser und Gärten um Wörlitz,* Leipzig, 1990

Baedeker's *Austria,* 2nd English edition

Baur, Max, *Das alte Potsdam,* Potsdam, 1991

Beer, Gretl, *Exploring Rural Austria,* Chicago, 1990

Berlitz Blueprint, *Germany,* Lausanne, 1991

Blunt, Anthony, *Baroque & Rococo,* New York, 1978

Bowe, Patrick, and Sapicha, Nicholas, *Gardens in Central Europe,* New York, 1991

Clausmeyer-Ewerc, and Modrow, Bernd, *Historische Gärten in Hessen,* Bad Homburg, 1989

Czerwenka, Fritz, *English: Hellbrunn,* Salzburg, 1991

Debrett, Cooper-Hewitt, Victoria and Albert Museum, *Designs for a Dream King,* London-New York, 1978

Fechtner, Harald, *Das alte Bad Homburg, 1870–1920,* Villingen-Schwenningen, 1977

Geirsberg, Hans-Joachim, and Hamm, Manfred, *Schlösser und Gärten in Potsdam,* Berlin 1991

Gumbel, Andrew, *Cadogan City Guides,* Berlin, London, 1991

Gunkel, Erich, *Bad Homburg: V. D. Hohe Impressionen einer Stadt,* Bad Homburg, 1990

Haiko, Peter, and Schezen, Roberto, *Vienna 1850–1930 Architecture,* New York, 1992

Hennebo, Dieter, et al, *Clemenswerth—Schloss im Emsland,* Bramsche, 1987

Hobhouse, Penelope, and Taylor, Patrick, *The Gardens of Europe,* New York, 1990

Hojer, Gerhard, *Die Amalienburg—Rokokojuwel im Nymphenburger Schlosspark,* Munich-Zurich, 1986

Jarry, Madelein, *Chinoiserie,* New York, 1981

Jellicoe, Geoffrey, *Baroque Gardens of Austria,* New York, 1932

Jellicoe, Geoffrey, and Jellicoe, Susan, *The Oxford Companion to Gardens,* Oxford-New York, 1986

Kempe, Lothar, Rossing, Renate, and Rossing, Roger, *Schlösser und Gärten um Dresden,* Leipzig, 1979

Kratzsch, Klaus, and Neumeister, Werner, *Sachsen und seine Geschichte,* Leipzig, 1990

Lehmann, John, and Bassett, Richard, *Vienna: A Traveller's Companion,* New York, 1988

Löffler, Fritz, *Der Zwinger zu Dresden,* Dresden, 1981

Man, John, and Sapieha, Nicolas, *Zwinger Palace Dresden,* London, 1990

Michelin Tourist Guide, *Germany—West Germany and Berlin,* Harrow, Middlesex, 7th edition, 1986

Michelin Tourist Guide, *Austria,* Harrow, Middlesex, 1st edition, 1992

Montgomery-Massingberd, Hugh, *Burke's Royal Palaces of Europe,* London, 1984

Mummenhoff, Karl E., *Schloss Nordkirchen,* Munich, 1979

Neidhardt, Hans Joachim, *Schloss Pillnitz,* Dresden, 1987

Von Richthofen, Christa, and Benn, Oliver, *Germany—Architecture, Interiors, Landscape, Gardens,* London, 1992

Seiler, Michael, *Das Palmenhaus auf der Pfaueninsel,* Berlin, 1989

Vienna Tourist Board, *Vienna from A to Z,* Vienna, 1989

## ACKNOWLEDGMENTS

We wish to thank the following for their assistance in the preparation of this book:

Esther Aall
Alfred Bush
Richard Day
Thomas Frangenberg
David Larsen
Brody Neuenschwander
Edith de Porada
Hilde Randolph
Charles Ryskamp
John Saumarez Smith
Princess Monica Ysenburg

*Sally Sample Aall*
*New York, 1994*

While traveling throughout Germany and Austria, two families provided me with invaluable support (and often a welcome bed for the night). In Germany, Prince and Princess Ysenburg, with their daughter Marguita, were very welcoming and helpful. Andreas and Lori Orsini-Rosenberg in Vienna proved to be faithful friends and often devoted their entire day to showing me the way to a secluded *lusthaus*. There were also many accommodating officials who went well beyond the call of duty to make it possible for me to photograph certain structures. During the several months it took me to complete this project, the kindness shown to me by those mentioned above—and many others—made my travels both stimulating and rewarding. Finally, I would like to express my special appreciation to Sally Sample Aall, who not only launched me on this adventure, but also introduced me to the special world of Follies and Fantasies. I have become such a convert that I am in the process of constructing a folly in our garden in Gloucestershire in the Cotswolds. To all those who made my work on this book such a pleasure, thank you.

*Nic Barlow*
*London, 1994*